NEW DIRECTIONS FOR COMMUNITY COLLEGES

Arthur M. Cohen
EDITOR-IN-CHIEF

Florence B. Brawer
ASSOCIATE EDITOR

Rekindling Minority Enrollment

Dan Angel
Austin Community College

Adriana Barrera
Austin Community College

EDITORS

Number 74, Summer 1991

JOSSEY-BASS INC., PUBLISHERS, San Francisco

MAXWELL MACMILLAN INTERNATIONAL PUBLISHING GROUP
New York • Oxford • Singapore • Sydney • Toronto

EDUCATIONAL RESOURCES INFORMATION CENTER

ERIC Clearinghouse For Junior Colleges

UNIVERSITY OF CALIFORNIA, LOS ANGELES

REKINDLING MINORITY ENROLLMENT
Dan Angel, Adriana Barrera (eds.)
New Directions for Community Colleges, no. 74
Volume XIX, number 2
Arthur M. Cohen, Editor-in-Chief
Florence B. Brawer, Associate Editor

Microfilm copies of issues and articles are available in 16mm and 35mm,
as well as microfiche in 105mm, through University Microfilms Inc., 300
North Zeeb Road, Ann Arbor, Michigan 48106.

LC 85-644753   ISSN 0194-3081   ISBN 1-55542-786-3

NEW DIRECTIONS FOR COMMUNITY COLLEGES is part of The Jossey-Bass
Higher and Adult Education Series and is published quarterly by Jossey-
Bass Inc., Publishers (publication number USPS 121-710) in association
with the ERIC Clearinghouse for Junior Colleges. Second-class postage
paid at San Francisco, California, and at additional mailing offices. Post-
master: Send address changes to Jossey-Bass Inc., Publishers, 350 San-
some Street, San Francisco, California 94104.

THE MATERIAL in this publication is based on work sponsored wholly or
in part by the Office of Educational Research and Improvement, U.S.
Department of Education, under contract number RI-88-062002. Its con-
tents do not necessarily reflect the views of the Department, or any other
agency of the U.S. Government.

EDITORIAL CORRESPONDENCE should be sent to the Editor-in-Chief,
Arthur M. Cohen, at the ERIC Clearinghouse for Junior Colleges, University of California, Los Angeles, California 90024.

Cover photograph by Rene Sheret, Los Angeles, California © 1990.

Printed on acid-free paper in the United States of America.

CONTENTS

INTRODUCTION

Increasing the rates of participation and success of minority students is one of the most important current goals of American higher education. Attaining that goal will benefit not only the groups directly affected, but our society as a whole. The national interest in this issue cannot be overstated. By the turn of the century, one of every three American school children will be members of minority groups; within a few more decades minorities will constitute one-third of the United States's total population. Through the year 2000, minority workers are expected to compose one-third of net additions to the work force. These statistics suggest a growing need to improve educational opportunities for blacks, Hispanics, Asian Americans, and American Indians.

Yet evidence shows that the pace of minority advancement has slowed since the significant achievements of the 1960s and early 1970s. In 1987 concern over reports of faltering progress prompted leaders of the American Council on Education (ACE) and the Education Commission of the States to form the Commission on Minority Participation in Education and American Life. The commission, made up of distinguished citizens from government, business, minority organizations, and higher education, spent six months reviewing relevant demographic and economic data and research and consulting with numerous experts in the field. It concluded that the nation was moving backward rather than forward in its efforts to integrate minorities into the life of the nation. Further, it challenged the nation to strive to erase the inequalities that characterize the lives of minority Americans, so that in twenty years an examination of similar data would reveal that minority citizens had attained a quality of life as high as that of the white majority.

Of course, this process will not be quick or easy, as recent findings on the educational attainment of minorities make clear. Statistics from ACE's Annual Status Report on Minorities in Higher Education show that, after improving for a number of years, high school completion among Hispanics declined dramatically between 1985 and 1989 (Carter and Wilson, 1991). During that period the rate for eighteen- to twenty-four-year-olds dropped from 62.8 percent to 56 percent. Among black Americans high school completion rates have improved little since the early 1980s, largely due to a stagnation in the rate for black men. And although Asian Americans complete high school at rates much higher than other ethnic groups, the overall figures mask wide disparities among subgroups. In 1980 only 22.3 percent of Hmong Americans and 31.4 percent of Laotian Americans over age twenty-five had completed high school.

These low—and in some cases declining—high school completion figures are major factors in the slow improvement in college participation by most minority groups in recent years. In some cases the situation has gotten even worse. The gap between Hispanic and white college participation has actually widened, and in 1989 only 16.1 percent of eighteen- to twenty-four-year-old Hispanics were enrolled in college. In 1988 the *number* of blacks enrolled in college reached an all-time high; however, over the last several years of the decade, blacks' rate of participation in higher education increased only slightly, and that increase was due exclusively to gains made by black women. Both Asian Americans and American Indians continue to be extremely underrepresented in higher education compared to their proportion of the U.S. population.

Because large numbers of minority students leave high school before completion, more of these young people end up seeking diplomas through the General Educational Development (GED) tests. In 1989, about one-third of candidates eighteen to forty-four years old were members of minority groups. Among all GED candidates, about one-third indicated that they planned to enroll in a community or junior college the following year. Such evidence suggests that community colleges need to be accessible to these students and be prepared to provide the kinds of support services required to help the students return to a traditional educational environment.

For minority students who aspire to continue beyond high school, community, junior, and technical colleges are an important gateway to higher education and a better quality of life. That fact helps account for the continuing strong expansion in community college enrollment at a time when the cohort of high school graduates is shrinking rapidly, and minorities constitute a growing share of that enrollment.

Research conducted by ACE found that in 1988 minorities composed 23 percent of the enrollment at community colleges, compared to 16 percent at four-year institutions (Carter, 1990). Minorities are more likely than whites to attend a two-year college. In 1988 46 percent of all minorities in higher education attended a community or junior college, compared to 36 percent of white students. Hispanic students especially remain concentrated in two-year institutions; 56 percent of those who continue past high school enroll in these schools. And the trend is accelerating. In the late 1980s Hispanic enrollment in community and junior colleges grew twice as fast as in four-year institutions.

In our rapidly changing economy those who attain only a high school education or less are burdened by significant and growing disadvantages. In this respect earning an associate degree can have major economic rewards, especially for blacks. Whereas the difference in median income between those with a high school diploma and those with an associate degree is 29 percent for the population as a whole, the disparity for blacks is 51 percent. The income difference between black bachelor's degree recipients and associate degree recipients is an additional 20 percent.

The latter figure demonstrates the importance of encouraging persistence and promoting the transfer of minority students from two- to four-year institutions. However, at present, transfer rates for Hispanics (23 percent) and blacks (18 percent) are far below the national average of 29 percent.

Recognizing this fact, with funding from the Ford Foundation, ACE formed the National Center for Academic Achievement and Transfer in the fall of 1989. The goal of the center is not merely to increase transfer activity but to raise the academic prospects of low-income students in urban areas.

During the first phase of the project, grants were awarded to partnerships of two- and four-year institutions with high concentrations of minority students in the twenty-five largest U.S. cities. The grants supported efforts by the partner colleges to collaborate more closely on academic activities designed to promote transfer. The center has also been developing a national transfer policy statement and conducting research, publishing and disseminating information, and examining legislative obstacles and opportunities. In the second phase of the project, the center will award grants to partner institutions to undertake development of joint core curricula that promote the movement of students from one school to another.

Our hope, of course, is that the projects sponsored by the center not only succeed at the partner institutions but serve as models to be emulated or adapted by hundreds of other colleges and universities. The ultimate measure of success will be whether we see an increased flow of minority students from community colleges to baccalaureate institutions and on through graduation, with all the options and opportunities such attainment affords.

But although transfer is of critical importance and must be encouraged, we also must remember that community colleges serve a vital function unrelated to the acquisition of degrees. In 1980 50 percent of two-year college students polled by the American Association of Community and Junior Colleges said that their primary reason for enrollment was to learn new job-related skills. With constant changes in technology, the increasing competitiveness of the international economy, and the aging of the U.S. population, continuing education will be a valuable key that can open doors to greater economic progress for persons of all groups.

Yet if access to educational opportunities for minorities does not improve—if we do not regain the momentum of the 1960s and 1970s—a disproportionate percentage of the members of these groups will continue to be condemned to lives of deprivation. Such a condition runs counter to our national ideals and threatens the foundation of our democratic system. Persistent inequities serve as a catalyst to social tensions and unrest. They also undermine our position in the global arena as both a moral force and an economic power.

As minority participation in the work force and other aspects of American life grows, we must begin to see minority citizens not as separate from the majority, but as a major component of the new America that will emerge in the next century. To prepare for that era, we must be willing to recommit ourselves to the goal of ensuring that all our citizens benefit from the prosperity and progress of the nation.

In this volume Dan Angel and Adriana Barrera provide an excellent review of the issues and challenges surrounding minority participation in community college education and of the initiatives being undertaken by a variety of organizations and institutions to promote it. These accounts are encouraging in that they demonstrate that efforts are being made in this area. However, they also serve as a graphic reminder of how much more must be done to ensure equal educational opportunity for the nation's minority citizens. Therefore, the best use to which readers can put this volume is not merely to absorb the information it presents but to devise ways in which they can adapt existing programs or develop new ones to meet the needs of their own institutions and students.

Robert H. Atwell
President
American Council on Education

References

Carter, D. J. "Community and Junior Colleges: A Recent Profile." *American Council on Education Research Briefs,* 1990, *1* (4).

Carter, D. J., and Wilson, R. *9th Annual Status Report on Minorities in Higher Education.* Washington, D.C.: American Council on Education, 1991.

Robert H. Atwell has been president of the American Council on Education (ACE) since December 1984. As president of ACE, Atwell is the leading spokesperson for American higher education on a broad range of public policy issues. He has been involved in efforts to preserve and expand federal funding for higher education and to increase educational opportunities for minority citizens.

Editors' Notes

According to a report issued by the American Association of Community and Junior Colleges and the Association of Community College Trustees (1990), minorities made up 22 percent of students enrolled in community, vocational, and junior colleges in the fall of 1986: 10 percent were black, 7 percent Hispanic, 4 percent Asian, and 1 percent Native American.

The figures are certainly not proportionate to the percentage of these groups within the U.S. population, and there is virtually unanimous agreement that within the next decade one-third of all Americans will be members of minority groups. The problems posed by these participation rates and demographic realities are reinforced by the global economic situation. In order to maintain our standard of living, the United States will have to develop a world-class work force. We can not reach that goal with a policy of de facto or de jure exclusion.

Our national record of success at minority participation in higher education seems to have abruptly ceased in 1978. Finally, in the late 1980s three major educational associations initiated significant efforts to rekindle minority participation in higher education. They have since been joined by hundreds of community colleges throughout America. This volume is focused on the efforts of these institutions and associations.

Chapter One provides a current snapshot of attempts to improve minority participation, using a review of the literature and the results of national survey data.

Chapters Two and Three deal with access. Raul Cardenas and Elizabeth Warren provide a general overview of the barriers to access and suggest a number of solutions. Roy G. Phillips assesses model access programs.

Chapters Four and Five examine recruitment. Anne E. Mulder focuses on recruiting obstacles and the means to remove them. Ronald A. Williams and Mary Anne Cox present a well-developed Connecticut state recruitment model program.

Chapters Six, Seven, and Eight are concerned with retention. James C. Henderson presents the relevant issues within a Native American context. David P. James, Mauro Chavez, and Margarita Maestas-Flores describe model programs successful with black and Hispanic students.

Chapters Nine, Ten, and Eleven deal with transfer. Louis W. Bender outlines state policy efforts. Judith S. Eaton focuses on the various treatments of transfer at community colleges, and Aram L. Terzian profiles an encouraging transfer opportunity program at the Community College of Philadelphia.

The crucial part of faculty and the administration role model are candidly discussed by J. Richard Gilliland in Chapter Twelve. Dale V. Gares and Exalton A. Delco, Jr., chronicle successful approaches at Austin Community College (Texas) in Chapter Thirteen.

Chapter Fourteen reviews the leadership provided by the American Council on Education, the Education Commission of the States, and the American Association of Community and Junior Colleges. Anyone seriously interested in the minority participation issue should examine the many publications from these sources, as well as the materials listed in Grace Quimbita and Anita Y. Colby's annotated bibliography (Chapter Fifteen).

The editors cannot conceive of an issue on the national higher education agenda deserving a higher priority than that of minority participation.

We have the need.

We have the knowledge.

Now is the time for action!

Dan Angel
Adriana Barrera
Editors

References

American Association of Community and Junior Colleges. *Where America Goes to College*. Washington, D.C.: American Association of Community and Junior Colleges, 1990.

Dan Angel is president of Austin Community College.

Adriana Barrera is assistant to the president at Austin Community College.

Activities to rekindle minority participation in community colleges are evidenced throughout the nation.

Minority Participation in Community Colleges: A Status Report

Adriana Barrera, Dan Angel

The introductory statement of *One-Third of a Nation* (American Council on Education and the Education Commission of the States, 1988, p. 1) notes, "America is moving backward—not forward—in its efforts to achieve the full participation of minority citizens in the life and prosperity of the nation." If this statement is true, the nation's community colleges must institute programs to reverse the current trend.

According to *Campus Trends, 1988* (El-Khawas), only one in four post-secondary institutions reported increased enrollment of black, Hispanic, or Native American students between the 1987 and 1988 academic years. The same report indicated that two-fifths of the administrators responding to the *Campus Trends* survey rated their institutions' ability to retain minority students as fair or poor.

Demographic projections, however, indicate that minority group populations are expected to increase more rapidly than the white population (Hodgkinson, 1985). Such an increase would not be alarming were it not for the fact that historically, as well as presently, the educational attainment of minority students has lagged behind that of their white counterparts.

That postsecondary institutions are concerned and actively involved in confronting the problems associated with minority student recruitment and retention is evidenced by the publication of *Minorities on Campus: A Handbook for Enhancing Diversity* (Green, 1989). But that publication includes seventy model practices, only three of which are associated with community colleges.

Based on these reports and on the consensus that minority students are more apt to attend two-year institutions of higher education than four-year colleges and universities, the editors of this book determined to assess the status of minority student participation in America's public community and junior colleges.

To do so, the editors conducted a literature search, surveyed the commissioners of higher education in each state, conducted a survey of a sample of community colleges nationwide, and identified implementers of promising programs.

A summary pertinent to each phase of the research will be presented.

Literature Search

A search of the ERIC database was conducted during the spring of 1989 that requested abstracts of articles submitted since 1980 on minority student participation in community colleges. The first purpose of this review was to provide data on minority student access, recruitment, retention, transfer, and attainment of educational goals. Another goal was to identify the researchers, as well as the implementers, of programs geared toward promoting minority student success. A second literature search examined articles published between March and December 1989.

Table 1 indicates the categories into which the articles from both literature searches were judged to belong. The categorization process followed a simple content analysis of the abstracts. Once completed, those categories that were rather limited in scope—that is, those containing fewer than five articles—were collapsed into broader categories. In two instances where the

Table 1. Categories Revealed by Literature Search

	1980–89	Mar.–Dec. 1989	Expected Number to Be Submitted for Nine Months
Institutional Categories			
1. Issues, trends, and demographic research	28	4	2
2. Self-assessment (service to minority students)	23	17	1.84
3. Basic skills instruction/ vocational education	22	2	1.76
4. Diversification of faculty and leadership	3	8	0.24
Student Categories			
1. Access/recruitment	20	9	1.60
2. Assessment	3	4	0.24
3. Retention/success	19	6	1.52
4. Transfer	30	2	2.4
Total	148	52	11.6

categories contained fewer than five articles but where the other labels did not capture their content, the original category labels (Student Assessment and Diversification of Faculty and Leadership) were retained.

A cursory examination of Table 1 shows that—with three exceptions—the nine months between March and December, 1989, were a prolific reporting period during which institutions assessed their own activities and services regarding women, minority, and disadvantaged students. This result surpassed expectations based on the previous nine years as recorded by the ERIC database.

These literature searches served to identify community college practitioners who could be tapped to provide specific information on their programs regarding minority students.

Survey of Commissioners of Higher Education

During September and October of 1989, the editors conducted a telephone survey of the commissioners of higher education in each state. The editors talked with the commissioner or a member of the commissioner's staff in thirty-four of the fifty states (68 percent). In two instances, the states did not have community colleges, and therefore the respondents could not assist in identifying exemplary programs in their states that dealt with minority student participation. Three state offices reported not having a sufficiently large minority population for which to develop specific programs. Of the remaining twenty-nine states, the staff of twelve commissioners' offices conveyed further information concerning particularly successful programs targeting minority students.

Unlike the literature searches, the telephone calls to the commissioners of higher education (or—if the position existed—to the commissioner for the community colleges division) revealed a general laissez faire attitude regarding minority student enrollments. Often two or three telephone calls were required before the person designated to answer these questions could be identified. Even then, the information available in the state offices was sketchy.

Nonetheless, of the twelve state offices that provided specific information, three furnished leads that developed into chapter contributions for this book.

Survey of Community Colleges

A questionnaire accompanied by a cover letter and self-addressed, stamped response card was mailed to 177 community college presidents. The cover letter from Dr. Dan Angel, president of Austin Community College, asked for assistance in identifying the administrators at each randomly selected college who could respond to questions regarding minority student enrollment and minority personnel employment practices and to programmatic questions regarding student support and academic services. This mailing resulted in the receipt of fifty-nine completed response cards for a response rate of 33 percent.

The questionnaire was then mailed with a second cover letter to the person named in the completed fifty-nine response cards as the chief institutional research officer. Followup mailings and telephone calls resulted in forty-six completed surveys, constituting 26 percent of the original sample. In fact, the completed surveys represented 82 percent of the completed response cards.

Eleven of the colleges that completed the survey reported an unduplicated head count of fewer than two thousand students; eighteen reported an unduplicated student head count of two to seven thousand students; and seventeen schools had unduplicated head counts greater than seven thousand students. Slightly more colleges reported having a majority of students enrolled in arts and science (N = 17) programs than in vocational technical programs (N = 11); eleven colleges reported fairly even enrollments in both types of programs.

The institutional profiles show that the colleges with fewer than two thousand students also reported less of an ethnic student mix than the larger colleges (see Table 2). Although minority students increased their enrollment in these colleges between 1983 and 1988, the pattern differed according to ethnic group. Regardless of college size, Asian students increased their enrollment dramatically; black student gains were more limited; Hispanic students decreased their enrollment in colleges with fewer than two thousand students but made substantial gains in larger institutions; and Native Americans decreased their enrollment in colleges with over seven thousand students but increased enrollment in colleges reporting fewer than seven thousand (see Table 3). These gains in minority student enrollment are tempered by the fact that white student enrollment grew across the board during the same period by an average of 34 percent. In order to have increased their relative

Table 2. Average Percent of Head Count by Ethnicity and College Size, Fall 1988

Ethnicity	Less than 2,000 Head Count (N = 11)	2,000–7,000 Head Count (N = 17)	7,000–30,000 Head Count (N = 17)
Asian	6.5	1.2	7.0
Black	3.5	5.2	7.2
Hispanic	1.2	16.4	7.5
Native American	1.6	1.8	0.5
White	86.8	74.0	74.0
Other	1.4	1.7	4.2
Total	101.0	100.3	100.4

Table 3. Percent Change in Unduplicated Head Count by Ethnicity and College Size, 1983–88

Ethnicity	< 2,000			2,000–7,000			7,000–30,000		
	1983	1988	Change	1983	1988	Change	1983	1988	Change
Asian	13	78	500%	385	776	101%	8,736	14,867	70%
Black	225	354	57%	3,188	3,326	4%	14,994	17,219	15%
Hispanic	108	98	-9%	8,215	10,453	27%	11,390	17,356	52%
Native American	178	198	11%	794	992	25%	1,345	1,274	-5%
White	6,248	8,661	39%	34,407	46,023	34%	153,917	196,512	28%
Other	60	28	-53%	813	869	7%	7,805	8,308	6%
Total	6,832	9,417	38%	47,802	62,439	31%	198,187	242,152	29%

college participation, enrollment by minority students must have outpaced that of white students. Unfortunately, at the colleges completing the survey, minority gains between 1983 and 1988 lagged behind that of white students (see Table 3).

Two areas that have been discussed in relation to minority student participation in higher education have been access to colleges from secondary school systems and transfer to four-year colleges and universities from community colleges. Overwhelmingly, the forty-six colleges reported articulation agreements in place with secondary school systems (76 percent) and four-year postsecondary institutions (91 percent).

Financial assistance to students by ethnic group was requested for the years 1983 and 1988. This information was rather difficult for most colleges to ascertain. Only a handful supplied data for both years; a few more reported the information for 1988 only. Several colleges wrote or called explaining that this type of detailed information is just now being recorded in an accessible manner. Because the information collected was fragmented, it is not reported in this chapter.

In examining minority student participation, it was also important to view changes in employment patterns according to ethnic group. Table 4 shows an increase in employment of all ethnic groups among the ranks of faculty, administrators, and professional-technical staff. These gains are relatively small, particularly when compared to the growth among white employee ranks.

Although the questionnaire used to collect these data was quite comprehensive in scope and detail, some information was readily accessible and some was not. Therefore, the responses to some of the questions posed (for example, regarding recruitment and retention) are not being reported here. The information was varied and in most instances did not yield to analysis.

Interviews with Implementers

The questionnaire did serve to identify some colleges that have or are developing promising programs. Some respondents sent brochures, pamphlets, news articles, and other items of information pertinent to the data collection. Additional contributors to this volume were also identified during this phase of the research.

A Note of Progress

Two years ago little was being reported about minority student participation in community colleges. However, discussions with practitioners across the nation and a review of the material accompanying the questionnaires indicate that many community colleges are taking action. Data are not always recorded in the same manner, and successes are not always published; how-

Table 4. Change in the Number of Personnel by Employment Classification, Ethnicity and College Size, 1983-88

Ethnicity	Faculty		Administrators		Prof/Tech	
	1983	1988	1983	1988	1983	1988
Asian	40	46	3	7	9	12
	44	86	8	11	11	38
Black	85	78	14	31	24	62
	147	207	27	43	53	101
Hispanic	98	112	22	51	201	289
	65	122	10	31	32	67
Native American	5	9	0	2	6	7
	5	18	0	1	1	8
White	1411	2206	258	446	328	719
	2674	3583	477	574	478	592
Other	2	3	1	1	1	1
	0	2	9	1	0	1

Note: For each ethnic group, the top row represents colleges with an unduplicated head count of fewer than 7,000 students; the bottom row represents colleges with an unduplicated head count greater than 7,000.

ever, activities to rekindle minority participation in community colleges are in evidence throughout the nation.

References

American Council on Education and Education Commission of the States. *One-Third of a Nation*. Washington, D.C.: American Council on Education, 1988. 47 pp. (ED 297 057)

El-Khawas, E. *Campus Trends, 1988*. Washington, D.C.: American Council on Education, 1988.

Green, M. F. *Minorities on Campus: A Handbook for Enhancing Diversity*. Washington, D.C.: American Council on Education, 1989.

Hodgkinson, H. L. *All One System: Demographics of Education—Kindergarten Through Graduate School*. Washington, D.C.: Institute for Educational Leadership, 1985. 22 pp. (ED 261 101)

Adriana Barrera is assistant to the president at Austin Community College, Austin, Texas.

Dan Angel is president of Austin Community College.

Community colleges provide a crucial link in the educational chain. Institutions must ensure that their policies and programs promote access for those who need it most.

Community College Access: Barriers and Bridges

Raul Cardenas, Elizabeth Warren

Open access to education is what distinguishes community colleges from all other educational institutions. It is through the community college commitment to access that the American dream of universal higher education is put into action and given substance. Community colleges have become expert at fitting into the context of people's lives and into the communities that they serve, both because of their proximity and because of the programs and services they offer.

The community college provides a special link in the educational chain. It serves as the only avenue to higher education for many minority students, older students, first-generation college students, and a number of others who may have dropped out of the educational mainstream. The community college provides a means for students to achieve their goals. Yet many students do not even make it through the open door, and those who do may still encounter barriers.

Fryer states that the primary strength of community colleges is "their uniquely American authenticity and congruity with this society's values" (1986, p. 19). The most effective community colleges are both mirrors and catalysts in their communities: they reflect the population and its values and strengths while at the same time providing educational services as a catalyst for change. To the extent that communities change, and some do very rapidly, there will always be challenges to access.

Maintaining open access and the range of programs that it requires is not only the most important service that community colleges offer, but it is also the most challenging. The key to preventing serious barriers to access at the institutional level is in always adapting to change. To react to change,

NEW DIRECTIONS FOR COMMUNITY COLLEGES, no. 74, Summer 1991 ©Jossey-Bass Inc., Publishers

the college must have accurate and continuous information about its community and its students. Just as important, it must be prepared to act on the information, a challenge that can be very difficult. Some institutions existing today were suburban "junior colleges" in the 1960s with predominantly white, 18-year-old, transfer-oriented populations. Twenty-five years later these same colleges have been transformed into urban "community colleges," trying to serve an adult population with vocational needs using the same aging faculty and out-of-date mission and goals. The irony for such community colleges is that they are being forced to react to changes that they in effect created by increasing the overall access to education in their communities.

Access and the Institution

Most community colleges have been in the position of responding to changes in the community and to the needs of its student population. In adapting to change so that access is preserved, the college must be prepared to examine and alter everything from the simplest telephone techniques to the mission of the institution. This chapter will assess challenges to access at the institutional level, provide some general recommendations on public policy, and describe some programs designed to insure that the concept of access remains meaningful.

The College Mission. The mission sets the expectations that both the college and the community have for the institution: that mission should create a climate that promotes access. If the mission is out of date, reflecting a time of different community and student needs, there will be a discrepancy between what the college is doing and what is needed. The mission must be reviewed at regular intervals to insure that it is still relevant. Other processes that derive from the mission, such as strategic, long-range, and budget planning, will suffer if the mission is obsolete. Even if the mission is broad enough to encompass changes in the community, a lack of vision, funding, motivation, or expertise will make it difficult to establish a process to support the necessary reforms. In an institution where there is a match between the mission and the needs of the community, the institutional priorities will reflect this congruence, and access will be preserved.

Funding. Institutional funding policies are usually built around the mission of the college and the needs of the community in order to maintain open access. In an environment of inadequate funding, these policies should support and protect on a priority basis those programs earmarked to serve minorities and other nontraditional college students and should insure that such programs are neither limited in scope, nor eliminated. Cohen comments that "state policies and funding formulas in large measure determine patterns of curriculum, student access, and eventually outcomes" (1987, p. 20). In addition, a decrease in student financial assistance will have a negative impact on minority and disadvantaged student enrollments. Federal, state, and institutional policies that place more of the burden on students to finance their education only serve to limit further access.

Assessment. An effective assessment program is built on the assumption that the institution has an option for students other than just rejecting them. Assessment can become a barrier when the process is used to limit access to certain programs or when there is inadequate programming to address the range of needs in the community. It can also prevent access when the assessment process is too mechanical, poorly presented, or generally insensitive to students, so that it itself becomes an impediment. The institution must insure that students are assessed, placed, and in general assisted in dealing with their educational needs.

Academic Placement. Closely related to assessment is the issue of placement. If the academic placement process is poorly developed and does not provide for remedial course work, it can serve as an obstacle to enrollment for those who need it most. The need to assess student strengths and weaknesses for placement purposes is very much a part of the everyday process. Colleges must be careful to assure that assessment instruments are used to determine appropriate placement and not to screen. Kanter shows that placement can be a barrier to underrepresented students: "In California's community colleges and in many two-year institutions across the nation, students are not 'admitted' to college in the formal sense. Instead, they are placed into courses as a result of assessment and directed into various levels of the community college curriculum. Thus, a parallel can be drawn between *placement* in an open access system and *admissions* in a closed or selective system" (1990, p. 10). Placement is an area that needs to be carefully monitored to insure that access is not being denied to minority and first-generation college students who are more prone to enter with lower skills.

Staff Development. An academic environment that supports access is one that provides academic readiness and facilitates student transition at a variety of levels and in a range of contexts. Colleges must provide preparation for faculty and staff so that they are prepared to meet the range of individual learning styles and student needs. Carefully designed and consistently funded faculty and staff development programs that promote cultural diversity are necessary to make certain that access is preserved. In addition, the curriculum and student services must be consistently monitored and adjusted to insure that they are current.

Articulation and Transfer. Problems with transfer and articulation have been consistent obstacles to access. The most common and persistent area of concern is the lack of articulated agreements between colleges and universities and even among community colleges themselves. There are often agreements in place that can facilitate the transfer of credits from institution to institution; however, much work remains to be done to smooth out and document the process for students. For many students, the community college is the only route to a four-year degree: when the transfer process is at best cumbersome, poorly coordinated, apathetic, or hostile, many minority and first-generation students opt out.

College/School Relationships. Coordination and articulation among all levels of education—from elementary through university—relates to curriculum, course competencies, course transfer, and adequate preparation of students. When institutions do not coordinate well, students repeat courses and lose credits and valuable time toward the degree, all of which can discourage students and ultimately affect access.

An important aspect of the college mission should be creating and maintaining open communications among all segments of the education system. Institutional connections between the links in the educational pipeline insure programming relevance, provide a more meaningful context for remediation, guarantee mutually complementary curricula, and facilitate transition. These linkages reinforce those institutional connections with the community necessary to keep the mission in focus and to preserve access. Inconsistent and poorly coordinated policies and procedures such as scheduling or course numbering—seemingly minor procedures from the institutional point of view—send confusing signals to students and directly limit access.

Student Support Services. Adequate student support services are critical to both access and retention. Institutional policies that limit these services create serious problems. Miller states that student services, in particular, "motivation, appropriate placement, realistic expectations about the nature of college life, support of academic performance, short- and long-term advising, and career counseling, are critically significant for fragile populations of learners" (1990, p. 8). Without these services students will find the adjustment to life in the institution problematic. Counseling and advising stand out as the most critical aspects of an effective student support system. Student support services must be valued highly by the institution in relation to its instructional offerings, because without them many students do not make it to the classroom.

Child care is also a constant concern for most adult students. The availability of child care services, which provide students an opportunity to attend classes while rearing their children, is an important part of a student support program that takes into account the whole context of students' lives.

Public Policy Impact on Access

Community colleges maintain access by responding to the requirements of their communities, but they are also bound by state and federal directives. Access problems can result when federal, state, and local policies are not coordinated, are poorly thought through, or are in direct conflict with one another and with community and student needs.

One example of counterproductive funding legislation is the Federal Vocational Education Act. This legislation restricts the access of the very students it purportedly intended to serve. As Prager describes it, the act " . . . restricts funding specifically sub-baccalaureate activity. This means that counseling services that would assist career students in transferring or curriculum articulation efforts between a community and a senior college (but not between community college and an area vocational and technical school) are precluded from fiscal support. Thus, a potentially powerful agent mandating the improvement of occupational-technical educational opportunity for the disadvantaged has built in provisos that limit the academic attainment of those whom it is designed to serve" (1988, p. 83).

Federal, state, and local governments can promote access through maintaining and improving funding and through coordinating broad policies to avoid problems like the one cited above. Below are some general recommendations on how public policies could be improved so that access is improved.

Funding for community colleges should be increased to insure that a broad range of academic, job training, and other services are provided for minority students. In addition, financial aid should cover the actual costs of attending college; otherwise the financial burden on students can be crippling and limit their ability to succeed.

As community colleges are part of a larger educational system or pipeline, funding for elementary and secondary schools must be improved to assure the retention and preparation of minority students.

States should mandate the coordination of data about students among and within education systems. States must also encourage coordination among institutions that promote transfer and retention.

States must be cautious about imposing policies that regulate assessment and testing, as they can impede rather than facilitate access.

Although the issue of transportation is rarely mentioned in the literature, it is a major consideration for most students. State and local governments must take into account students' physical access to colleges and other educational institutions when transportation plans are developed.

Community colleges serve many students with families. Single parents, in particular, are often unable to achieve their educational goals because of inadequate child care. The state and federal government must furnish adequate funding for child care for those who need it, especially those who are pursuing educational objectives.

Programs That Promote Access

The first part of this chapter has described the need to improve and develop programs that broaden the relationships among all segments of the educational community so that policy and procedures do not become barriers to student access. Programs are now being developed around the nation designed to promote and maintain access to higher education for minority students. The programs highlighted here are just a few of those within the Maricopa Community College District (Phoenix, Arizona) that address some of the problems described above. These are programs specifically designed to insure that policies and programs facilitate access to education.

Think Tank. The Think Tank is a consortium of educational institutions representing the educational continuum from kindergarten through the community college. It represents a unique opportunity for substantial, positive changes in the delivery of educational services to the residents of the city of Phoenix. Together, the participating institutions combine their expertise, support their respective initiatives, and coordinate the delivery of services to improve the potential and the quality of the lives of the students they serve. The members of the consortium have made a commitment to develop longitudinal programs that may take from ten to fifteen years to yield results. The programs being developed through the Think Tank are being organized into a model that will "wrap around" students to promote academic success (Jordan, 1990).

Achieving a College Education. The goal of the Achieving a College Education (ACE) program is to increase the numbers of students who achieve baccalaureate degrees after successfully completing high school and community college degrees. ACE is geared to students who make average grades but who are at risk of not completing high school. Students are recruited in the second semester of their sophomore year of high school and are involved continuously with the college from that point onward. Parental involvement and preparation are stressed throughout the program. Students are oriented to postsecondary education and provided with the academic and social skills necessary to survive in that environment. The program is based on overlapping the community college experience with the high school on one end and the community college with the university on the other to eliminate the gaps between institutions. Students have the opportunity to experience the next level of education while they are still in a comfortable, familiar environment.

Urban Teacher Corps Partnership. With the dramatic demographic changes taking place in our public school population, the need for minority representation on faculties is evident. The shortage of qualified minority and bilingual teachers has been identified as a critical problem for Phoenix's elementary, secondary, and postsecondary schools. The Urban Teacher Corps Partnership (UTCP) is addressing this concern by structuring a program for instructional aid so that prospective minority teachers can pursue their education. The UTCP program enables teacher candidates to participate in an ongoing, structured study/support group program and to complete a baccalaureate degree and obtain teacher certification. The program offers on-site classes at the school districts and provides child care, transportation, mentors, teleconferencing, computer-based learning (where possible), and ongoing group support. The UTCP emphasizes preparation for and assistance with transfer and adjustment to higher education. It also focuses on developing the teachers' commitment to teach in the inner city. The program consists of blocks of required courses at the community college and university. Candidates have the opportunity to pursue individual specialties and interest areas through elective courses.

Student Monitoring and Alert System. In an effort to follow up on the students enrolled in ACE and similar programs, the Student Monitoring and Alert System (SMASh) was developed. SMASh has been designed to work under a fourth-generation, relational data base management system with links to existing student data systems at the Maricopa Community Colleges and the Phoenix Union High School District. Plans are under way to include elementary schools in the system as well.

SMASh functions as a student-progress monitoring and early-alert system that combines current, dynamic information from public schools and postsecondary institutions. The system allows longitudinal comparisons of program, group, and individual student performance so that timely and effective interventions can be planned. With the unique data-sharing agreements that exist among the participating institutions, SMASh will be able to provide extensive information on student activity (both curricular and noncurricular) so that sound decisions can be made allowing both students and programs to fulfill their true potential.

Conclusion

Barriers to access to higher education are not likely to disappear easily. The reality for community colleges is that they will serve an increasingly urban, younger, and minority population, as well as one more financially dependent. Preserving access depends on the colleges' ability to adapt to changing community needs, to evaluate and adjust institutional practices, and to continue to monitor and influence policymakers.

References

Cohen, A. "Facilitating Degree Achievement by Minorities: The Community College Environment." Paper presented at the conference "From Access to Achievement: Strategies for Urban Institutions." Los Angeles, Nov. 15–17, 1987. 37 pp. (ED 283 576)

Fryer, T. "Some Tough Questions About Community Colleges." *Community and Junior College Journal*, 1986, 56 (6), 18–21.

Jordan, N. "Think Tank Educational Consortium." Phoenix, Ariz.: Maricopa Community College District, 1990.

Kanter, M. "Is Placement a Barrier to Access for Underrepresented Students in Community Colleges?" *Community College Week*, 1990, 2 (18), 10–11.

Miller, C. "Minority Student Achievement: A Comprehensive Report." *Journal of Developmental Education,* 1990, *13* (3), 6–11.

Prager, C. "The Other Transfer Degree." In C. Prager (ed.), *Enhancing Articulation and Transfer.* New Directions for Community Colleges, no. 61. San Francisco: Jossey Bass, 1988.

Raul Cardenas is the founding president of South Mountain Community College, one of the Maricopa Community Colleges, in Phoenix, Arizona.

Elizabeth Warren is manager of the Think Tank at the Maricopa Community Colleges office.

In addition to its traditional function, a higher education system should be judged by its ability to increase the pool of well-prepared minority students.

Model Programs in Minority Access

Roy G. Phillips

A review of the literature regarding the access of minority groups, including blacks, Hispanics, and Native Americans, indicates that they continue to be underrepresented in higher education and the professions. This underrepresentation has created a national urgency to enlarge the pool of well-prepared minority students in order to improve the productive capacity of our nation within an increasingly competitive global economy. Moreover, because minority students are concentrated in the community colleges of the nation, the role of the community college system—especially its success in promoting transfers to four-year institutions—becomes a paramount issue in this decade and beyond.

Introduction

The purpose of this chapter is to assess model programs in minority access and to discuss their implications for new directions in community college education. For purposes of definition, the concept of *minority access* shall be confined to mean the admission of students whose academic performance may have been compromised by inadequate preparation, resources, and support (Birnbaum, 1987). By this definition the concept of access is separate from that of academic quality as gauged by such standards as SAT scores.

Overview of Trends and Issues

Legal Basis for Access. The legality of equal access to public secondary and higher education in America has its basis within the liberal tradition of the American education system. This tradition was reaffirmed by the 1954 Brown decision and the 1960s civil rights laws passed by the United States Congress. Although the civil rights legislation of the 1960s was designed to redress the historic exclusion of blacks from access to the public secondary and higher education institutions, it also provided the legal foundation for the inclusion of other disenfranchised American minorities, including Asians, Hispanics, and Native Americans. The effect of the 1960s civil rights legislation was to refocus national attention on the egalitarian function of education (Astin, 1982).

The decade of the 1960s showed promise for access to higher education by minorities. As a general trend, enrollment in higher education between 1976 and 1986 increased 13.8 percent. Enrollment of minority students in higher education during that period increased significantly. Between 1984 and 1986, the enrollment of minorities increased by 7.6 percent (American Council on Education, 1988). By the middle of the 1980s, however, a new policy agenda arose in higher education. The new policy agenda was reflected in the Defunis and Bakke cases and the educational reform movement of the middle and late 1970s.

As a consequence of the Bakke decision and the emerging educational reform movement initiated through an assessment of our public schools in *A Nation at Risk,* the tension between quality and access heightened (Birnbaum, 1987). A renewed concern for quality resulted in the restriction of access based on relative achievement on standardized tests. Furthermore, this renewed concern for quality was simultaneous with a reduction of minority enrollment and the waning of public interest in the question of minority access.

Impact of a Changing Environment. Since the end of World War II, changes within the American economy have retarded the access and mobility of an increasing number of minorities, especially those who were not able to gain from the economic expansion of the post–World War II era. Several trends have added to the plight of poor and disadvantaged minorities. First, the American economy has become increasingly global. The nation no longer wields the dominant economic power over the global market place. It faces intense international competition from other emerging industrialized nations. Second, structural changes are taking place within the American work place. Highly influenced by increasing world competition and an emerging information-based technology that requires less energy, the country is now moving toward a radical transformation of its occupational and income structure (McKee, 1985). Old-line users of steel, transportation, textiles, and rubber have declined. Some phases of production are moving abroad where cheaper, nonunionized labor is more available. As a consequence, the nation's job structure and new educational requirements have curtailed the prospects for equal access and social mobility for those who occupy the bottom tier of the income and occupational pyramid. Third, a new and different immigration trend has emerged in the last two decades. Immigrants from Latin America and Asia have accounted for more than three-fourths of all legal immigration during the 1970s (McKee, 1985). The second wave of the new immigrants has been mainly unskilled minorities who have settled in the large urban centers of the nation and compete for jobs and other declining resources with an increasingly disadvantaged black population.

Birnbaum (1987) indicates that the multiplying impact of these trends has added a new dimension to the politics of quality and access: "Resources of all kinds are always limited; and time, attention, political support, and money are devoted to one item on the agenda—whether the agenda of public policy or that of an academic institution—are not available to another" (p. 3). The limited federal resources have shifted many traditional federal responsibilities to the state and local governments. As a consequence, Birnbaum (1987, p. 3) further asserts: "A preoccupation with access during the earlier period has been replaced today by a consuming interest in quality, and it has not appeared possible to attend to both." A review of this dilemma will provide some understanding of the increasing impact of state policymakers attempting to respond to the conflicting needs of access and quality.

An Assessment of Model Programs in Minority Access

Assessment Criteria. Astin describes a number of factors affecting minority access. These will be used to assess the quality of model programs in minority access that have been surveyed in the literature. Astin's factors are summarized in four major areas: academic preparation, career planning, positive reference-group expectancy, and institutional and financial assistance (1982).

The literature confirms that the quality of the students' academic preparation at the time of college entry has the greatest impact on access and success of any single measure (Astin, 1982). High school grades, aptitude test scores, study habits, and the nature of the subjects taken are positively related to persistence for minority students. The student's initial choice of career goals and plans shows a substantial relationship to undergraduate grade-point average and persistence. Career-goal-directed students tend to be highly motivated and self-directed in higher education. In addition, high expectations communicated by parents, teachers, peers, and significant others provide a positive group expectancy. The message from these groups is powerful in that it communicates, either verbally or nonverbally, the level of performance that is expected. The impact of institutional climate and financial assistance measures are also significantly related to college persistence of minority students. Comprehensive support services such as tutoring and work study, on-campus residency, and faculty attitudes are contributing factors.

Minority programs that incorporate these factors promote high rates of student success. The research literature describes the impact of these programs. The characteristics of four model programs will be discussed in the following categories: an early intervention strategy, a transfer strategy, and a retention strategy.

An Early Intervention Strategy. An early intervention strategy in Florida is described by Phillips (1988). The two programs are called the Miami Promise and the Black Student Opportunity Program, both developed and implemented in 1987. They were designed as a partnership among Miami–Dade Community College, the Urban League of Greater Miami, the Dade County Public Schools, the United Teachers of Dade, and the Mitchell Wolfson Senior Foundation. The major goal of the two programs is to increase the college attendance of well-prepared black students.

Miami Promise is an early intervention academic preparation program at the elementary school level that has received nationwide attention. The current program is housed at the Dade County Charles Drew Elementary School. Approximately sixty-two sixth-grade students were selected.

The Black Student Opportunity Program is an early intervention academic preparation program at the senior high school level. The current program is housed within two Dade County public schools: Northwestern Senior High School, a predominantly black high school, and Southridge Senior High School, an integrated school located in the south Dade County community.

Students within the two programs were selected based upon the following criteria: standardized test achievement in the middle stanine range (5-6) of the Stanford Achievement; a 2.0 grade-point average; parent participation; student participation in after-school and Saturday tutorial sessions; and student participation in motivational, time-management, study-skills, and self-management workshops. Students are also required to enroll in the essential academic disciplines that improve information skills: in mathematics, science, English, social science, and computer literacy.

In addition to the academic preparation component, the program contains three others. The first provides scholarship assistance based upon incentives for achievement. Funds are raised for each student by a sponsor. Based upon the student's achievement, beginning at the ninth-grade level, he/she is able to earn dollars for letter grades in each of the basic disciplines computed on an annual basis; for each *C*, $30 is placed in the student's account; for each *B*, $60; and for each *A*, $90. The incentive scholarship level is increased as students enter and complete the first two years at Miami–Dade Community College. These earnings are matched by the Mitchell Wolfson Senior Foundation on a one-to-one basis. In effect, each student has the potential for earning $3,000 or more from high school through the college sophomore year. The second component is an articulation agreement that has been worked out with four-year colleges and universities that agree to participate in the program. Essentially, the four-year postsecondary institutions have agreed to establish scholarship and/or financial aid assistance for those students who graduate from Miami–Dade and enroll in their respective institutions. The third component is a program that assigns a mentor to work with students individually and with their parents or guardians. This component is designed to increase positive group expectancy and role modeling to facilitate success. An individualized computerized program has been established to monitor each student's progress and to send letters to the students and their parents alerting them to any problems of academic deficiency.

The impact of the program at this writing is encouraging. Fourteen of the senior high school participants graduated in 1989. Two of the students chose to enter the military, and the remainder are enrolled in college. The remaining senior high school students are expected to graduate in 1990. All of the elementary population are still enrolled at the ninth grade level.

A Transfer Strategy. Rendón and Matthews (1989) report on a model minority retention strategy program that has proven to have a positive impact upon high-risk students. The model is referred to as the Middle School, carefully patterned after the Middle College High School at La Guardia Community College in New York. The Middle College embodies the concept of an alternative high school and two-year college. Only high-risk students in the tenth grade are recruited to attend Middle College. They are required to take the next three years of schooling at the college site. The following components are included as a part of the model: internship work experience, career planning, personal counseling, and the opportunity to repeat courses without stigma of failure. The program reports an 85 percent graduation rate and 75 percent attendance rate. The strong articulation between the high school and the college encourages smooth transfer.

Similarly, Elvin and Wood (1989) cite a unique model program in minority transfer. The program involves twenty-five two-year institutions paired with a similar number of four-year colleges and universities. The program is funded by the Ford Foundation and is called the Urban Community College Transfer program. It was developed out of national concern to increase the minority student transfer rate primarily between community colleges and four-year colleges and universities. The program focuses on an early identification of high-risk high school students with potential, emphasis upon academic preparation in the essential college preparatory disciplines, and formulation of articulation agreements between community colleges and four-year institutions.

A Retention Strategy. Mese and Spano (1989) describe a model retention program developed at Miami–Dade Community College/Medical Center Campus. The campus program is mainly in the nursing and allied health areas. Approximately 70 percent of the entering students require remediation in at least one of the basic skills areas. A rigorous curriculum is in place to prepare each student to pass state-administered certification requirements. The program stresses a counselor/mentor relationship, an alert system to provide immediate student feedback on academic progress, an integrated system of academic support services to assist students in need, and personalized communication and a nurturing environment designed to remove emotional barriers to learning. The program has resulted in a 95 percent success rate on state certification examinations in the allied health areas.

These model programs in minority access set trends that have broad implications for improving minority enrollments and achievement in higher education. They will provide the basis for future minority access programs.

An Emerging Agenda in Minority Access

The issue of increasing minority access and achievement has emerged as a high-priority agenda item for the 1990s. Hodgkinson stresses the rationale for this urgency (1985, p. 7): "Most important, by around the year 2000, America will be a nation in which one of three of us will be nonwhite. And minorities will cover a broader socioeconomic range than ever before, making simplistic treatment of their needs even less useful." The meaningful participation of minorities in the social, political, and economic leadership of the nation will require that they persist in higher education. To accomplish this presents an exceptional challenge to community colleges, where the majority of minority students are enrolled. From a review of the literature, it is clear that certain trends will continue into the next decade and beyond.

First, it is clear that the issue of quality and access will continue to dominate the higher education agenda for the next decade. This observation is supported by Birnbaum (1987, p. 19): "The genius of American higher education is that it attempts to a degree not found elsewhere in the world, to support both quality and access. And indeed, in our educational system, neither quality nor access can survive alone; it is only in combination that they define our educational system." Second, although there is an important role for the federal government to play in the provision of minority access to higher education, the responsibility will continue to shift to the states as efforts to reduce the federal budget deficit grow. Focusing attention on the role of the states appears particularly appropriate in this decade and beyond. States recognize the reality of changing demographics as they seek to compete with each other and with other nations for new jobs and economic growth. Third, as states become more involved in the development of policy initiatives to improve minority access, they will require greater accountability through monitoring the progress of local educational institutions. Requirements for the establishment of more formalized partnerships among public secondary schools, two-year institutions, and four-year colleges and universities will increase. Fourth, there is a growing consciousness by some minority groups, especially blacks, that current programs in minority access only marginally enlarge their numbers in the higher education pipeline. As a consequence, black organizations, including churches, business associations, and civic and fraternal groups, are taking greater responsibility for minority student access (Phillips, 1988). This trend will continue into the next decade and beyond. Fifth, the private business community will become more involved in the development of quality and access programs for minorities.

The private sector views education as a capital investment for the future success of America within an increasingly competitive global economy. This observation is best exemplified in a statement by Donley ("Education: A Capital Investment," 1987, p. 92): "I am committed to education as a businessman because it is, quite simply, America's most important enterprise. The quality of our educational system translates, in large measure, into the quality of our people, our work force, the main engine that runs our industrial complex." Community colleges in America have an opportunity to position themselves at the leading edge of this emerging agenda.

References

American Council on Education. *Minorities in Higher Education: Seventh Annual Status Report.* Washington, D.C.: American Council on Education, 1988.

Astin, A. W. *Minorities in American Higher Education: Recent Trends, Current Prospects, and Recommendations.* San Francisco: Jossey-Bass, 1982.

Birnbaum, R. "Administrative Commitments and Minority Enrollments: College President's Goals for Quality and Access." *Review of Higher Education,* 1987, *11* (4), 19, 35-57.

"Education: A Capital Investment." *Business Week,* June 22, 1987, p. 92.

Elvin, R. S., and Wood, G. L. "AAU Research Institution Pilots Transfer Institute to Enhance Minority Educational Opportunities." Unpublished manuscript, 1989. 30 pp. (ED 308 921)

Hodgkinson, H. L. *All One System: Demographics of Education—Kindergarten Through Graduate School.* Washington, D.C.: Institute for Educational Leadership, 1985. 22 pp. (ED 261 101)

McKee, J. B. "Race, Ethnicity and Religion in a Changing America. Observation for the 1980's." Paper presented at the National Conference of Christians and Jews, New York, N.Y., 1985.

Mese, J. H., and Spano, C. M. "Retention Through Intervention: A Strategic Plan for Retention of High-Risk Students." Paper presented at the 11th Annual International Conference on Teaching Excellence and Conference of Administrators, Austin, Tex. May 21-24, 1989. 35 pp. (ED 305 978)

Phillips, R. G. *Partners in Education: Black Student Opportunity Program.* Miami, Fl.: Miami–Dade Community College District, 1988. 60 pp. (ED 298 691)

Rendón, L. I., and Matthews, T. B. "Success of Community College Students: Current Issues." *Education and Urban Society,* 1989, *21* (3), 312-327.

Roy G. Phillips is the founding vice-president of the Homestead Campus of Miami–Dade Community College, Homestead, Florida.

Recruitment of minority students centers less on issues related to academic preparedness and financial support than on questions related to institutional environment.

Minority Student Recruitment

Anne E. Mulder

An *open door*? A *closed door*? A *revolving door*? What term accurately reflects the efforts of community colleges in attracting minority students to their campuses? The question is being posed by community colleges across the country as they examine their effectiveness in attracting and assisting minority students in achieving their educational goals. Though the problems and the solutions for recruitment initiatives may vary, minority student concerns related to academic preparedness and financial resources, as well as issues concerning institutional climate, are found on each campus. And it is vital that community colleges confront these problems *now*. Preparing for the student body of the 1990s and into the twenty-first century demands identifying and analyzing the barriers to access and equity for minority students entering community colleges. Moreover, developing positive guidelines for recruitment initiatives that enhance rather than inhibit the open door philosophy is a necessity.

Identifying the Barriers

Much of the literature regarding minority access to and success in postsecondary institutions focuses on the four-year institution. Although the community college varies both structurally and philosophically from this setting, some insight can be gained from the available research. Unique variables may exist, but three general concerns for the majority of institutions have been identified: academic preparedness, the availability of financial resources, and the prevailing institutional climate. The success or failure of minority recruitment initiatives seems directly related to how well the institution assesses and addresses these concerns.

A variety of sources—definitive studies prepared by national and state commissions, academic journals, and popular magazines—have presented the predicament of unprepared or underprepared students entering college. Though the problem is not confined to any one ethnic group, the impact of the lack of preparedness may be most severe in the case of minority students aspiring to higher education. The issues involved may be examined from a variety of perspectives. These include differences in the academic opportunities of racial groups that can be traced to inadequate curricula, linguistic difficulties, and family concerns. A study carried out by a joint task force of the Michigan State Board of Education and the Michigan Equal Employment Opportunity Council (Michigan Department of Education, 1986) identifies areas such as inadequate math and writing instruction, improper counseling, and program placement, as well as racial prejudice, as barriers affecting the college admission of minority high school graduates. Differences in the quality of academic preparation of the white and black college-going population and an increasing percentage of black high school dropouts have been cited as reasons for the decline in minority enrollment. Problems are exacerbated for Hispanic students, who not only experience basic linguistic obstacles but are simultaneously confronted with having to function in specific content-area courses in a solely English environment (Edwards, 1986). Recent studies have pointed to the importance of self-image, family involvement, and expectations for success as essential components of academic preparedness (Kalamazoo Valley Community College, 1988).

A growing body of literature points to the general area of financial need as another barrier to minority student recruitment. Evans (1985) noted several converging factors, including the availability of and eligibility for federal financial aid, the lack of student confidence in the financial return on college investment, and movement away from affirmative action and civil rights initiatives at the federal level, as the basis of financial concerns. Ironically, current and potential minority college students are increasingly dependent upon financial aid at a time when the number of real dollars available is shrinking. The situation is further aggravated by the complicated procedures tied to financial aid applications, as well as by the prospect of greater student indebtedness as a result of growing emphasis on loans (Kalamazoo Valley Community College, 1988).

A final barrier to minority recruitment centers less on the reality of the student's experience than on the student's perception of the institution. Institutional environment is particularly germane to a student's college selection process. One study (Simpson, 1987) noted that blatant racial incidents have less impact upon the attraction and retention of minorities than other more subtle forms of racism, such as exclusion from study groups, insecurity about the admissions process, and the perception of nonminorities on campus that lower standards are used in the admission of minority students. Fleming (1984) cites several factors inherent in a positive instructional environment: the opportunities for peer relationships and role models, the possibility of participating in campus life, the presence of other minority students, curricula relevant to the minority experience, and responsive counseling services. Clearly, most authors believe strongly in the effect of institutional environment on the ability of a college to attract the minority student.

For the community college, then, to become a truly barrier-free institution for the minority student, three factors must be carefully evaluated. First of all, the institution must determine its responsiveness to issues surrounding the academic preparedness of the students to be served. Second, the college must explore the availability of financing for the students desiring an education. Third, internal conditions that foster a positive climate must be assessed and created.

Overcoming the Barriers

In recruiting minority students, how can an institution respond to problems of academic preparedness? How can opportunities for financial aid be improved? How can a responsive institutional climate be achieved? Assuredly, many traditional approaches to these problems should continue. Tutorial programs for at-risk students, increased scholarships directed toward minority students, and continuous audits of the institutional environment are essential. Recruitment initiatives, however, should recognize the conceptual and practical linkages within a student's intellectual, personal, and social development; hence, many community colleges are now developing creative early intervention programs designed to identify students from elementary and secondary schools who lack motivation or adequate preparation for college. These programs have been designed to provide additional assistance after school or during the summer. Some have featured early placement testing paired with specialized instruction. Others are geared toward specific curricula. All of them closely link parents, partnerships with the schools, and involvement with the community.

At Lake Michigan College in Benton Harbor, Michigan, two early intervention programs have been implemented. One of the programs, funded in cooperation with the Whirlpool Foundation, focuses on seventy-six inner-city youth who have been promised a scholarship to the college upon their high school graduation. Sixty-two of these children are black. An important aspect of the program is the sponsorship of individual students by volunteer faculty, staff, and community members. Sponsors are responsible for contacting their students at least once a month. The students spend time at the college and attend summer camps and various programs during the school year to complement their regular school activities. Now in its third year of operation, the program has been adopted by several other community colleges in Michigan and Illinois.

Another early intervention program entitled Mini-Met at Lake Michigan College is an offspring of the highly successful Michigan Educational Trust program (MET), instituted by the state of Michigan. The program provides a guarantee of today's tuition prices for tomorrow's education to parents who invest now. The college has modified the program for students in one of the rural school districts served by the college. In this predominately black district, only about 20 percent of the high school graduates now go on to college. Many of them could not afford the financial investment required by the state's program; however, some eighty elementary students have enrolled in the Mini-Met program, paying installments of $3 per week. The students' weekly savings are collected at the school, and a local bank serves as the holding agent. The program has worked out contingencies including refunds with interest for children who choose another college, receive a scholarship, or decide not to go to college at all. Furthermore, families can choose options such as completing their financial obligation early or purchasing two years of college instead of just one. Although the program may emphasize one institution, the students are still encouraged to think about college as an option and to keep that goal in mind throughout the remainder of their elementary-secondary-school years.

Other colleges are addressing compelling special needs in appealing to minority recruits. Wayne County Community College in Detroit, Michigan, has instituted the Urban Teacher Program, designed to recruit teachers from minority groups through partnerships between four-year institutions and community colleges. Currently, some seventy students, primarily older black adults, are enrolled. As part of the program's design to familiarize the participants with the urban classroom, the students will have completed several semesters of field work in Detroit-area schools under the guidance of mentor teachers prior to receiving their associate's degrees. Supported by grants from the Michigan legislature, the state education department's office of minority equity, and the Fund for the Improvement of Postsecondary Education, the program will enroll some three hundred students by the end of its third year. Not only is it an innovative recruitment initiative, but the program also provides an opportunity for meaningful articulation between the community college and the four-year college while addressing the critical problem of the shortage of minority teachers.

Though early intervention programs and creative recruiting initiatives may assist specific minority students, a serious issue for many minorities resides in the financial obligations of college matriculation. The importance of finances appears even more pronounced for minority adults. A Kalamazoo Valley Community College study (1988) identified the cost of tuition and books, as well as a general inability to meet additional expenses incurred by attending college, as particularly significant to black and Hispanic students. Responsible recruitment initiatives must include financial counseling for minority students: colleges must provide information that will prevent the students from making decisions about burdensome loan payments that may deter their remaining in school. Furthermore, colleges need to consider institutional policies that minimize a student's dollar investment. A simple review of the frequency of textbook changes and an examination of the cost of books for specific subject areas as compared to other local institutions might alleviate some financial difficulties.

As we have noted, a supportive institutional environment is essential to successful minority student recruitment. A minority presence on a college's board of trustees, within its faculty and staff ranks, and in an office or council specifically concerned with minority affairs provides a structural response to environmental concerns. Mentor programs that include student, staff, and community volunteers offer an opportunity for minority students to come into contact with role models. Campus activities that involve both minority and other students not only increase the participation of minority students, but they also enrich campus life in general. Staff in-service training focusing on ethnic and cultural diversity is mandatory for an understanding of minority concerns and perceptions about the institution. All these initiatives are essential for creating a positive institutional environment.

Developing Positive Guidelines

Faced with a growing number of minority students who need postsecondary education and, simultaneously, with an increasing array of issues confronting both students and institutions, community colleges must aggressively evaluate their minority recruitment initiatives. An institution truly committed to this endeavor can use five guidelines to assess their performance.

1. *Clarify the Motivation.* Institutions need to affirm why they believe minority recruitment is important. Placating a broader community concern, addressing social issues, developing a work force, and being morally responsible are all sound reasons, to be sure. But the reality is that the number of minority students attending community colleges has the potential to increase rapidly well into the twenty-first century. To survive, a community college must respond to that client group.

2. *Develop the Vision.* Developing vision is essentially heightening sensitivity to the needs of the minority students enrolled within the institution and creating an institutional environment where students are presented with a mandate to succeed, not the right to fail. Such a climate assumes attitudinal and structural changes within the institution. It assumes as well that diversity is viewed as healthy and that empowerment is the right of every individual, not a selected few.

3. *Audit the College Culture.* If the goal is to create an institutional climate that will attract minority students, then the first important step may be to determine what the present culture is or, equally as important, how it

is perceived by minority students. There is a great body of unspoken and unexamined assumptions, values, and mythologies that define an institution; thus, it may be difficult for a college to conduct a successful audit without outside assistance. An assessment should be a research activity that relies on extensive in-depth interviews and a lot of listening.

The operative institutional assumptions must be identified and evaluated, but they are sometimes terribly uncomfortable to confront. Institutional culture is like a tree. Its roots are assumptions about the college and about the world. Its branches, leaves, and seeds are the behavior manifested by students, faculty, and staff. The leaves cannot be altered without changing the roots: peaches cannot grow on an oak. Or rather, with the proper grafting, peaches *can* grow on an oak, but they come out much like acorns—small and hard and not appealing to eat. To grow good fruit, a tree must have the proper roots.

4. *Modify the Assumptions.* The real problem with the institutional culture tree is that terrible opposition occurs when fundamental change is attempted. Every culture, including that of a community college, has defensive elements that turn out in force every time a basic assumption is threatened. We cannot assume we are one big family; we cannot assume we are a melting pot; we cannot assume people are all motivated the same way or learn the same way. We must learn to embrace diversity both in the systems we create and in the people we recruit.

5. *Create the Responsive System.* The responsive system means, first of all, modifying existing structures. It means, as well, having in place models that emulate the vision, models that represent the culture. It means dealing internally with the root causes of prejudice and inequality. It means creating an environment that can develop the full potential of every student who comes to the institution. It means living with reality: diversity. It can be the greatest strength.

A Final Word

In a recent study by the Education Commission of the States and the State Higher Education Executive Officers, Callan focuses on the dilemma confronting recruitment, retention, and the graduation of minorities from postsecondary institutions. He points out that all too often, "The institutions which collect the data, the states which compile it and the federal government which reports it—have approached the issue from a 'compliance' perspective." He responds, "This is not enough. Commitment, not compliance will be needed to turn the American dream into an American reality" (Mingle, 1987, p. 8). Clearly, rekindling the minority student participation in America's community colleges will demand an unquestionable commitment. It will also demand, not the rhetoric of compliance, but the reality of action that assures that the open door remains open.

References

Edwards, F. L. "Barriers to Hispanics in Higher Education or 'Is There Life After ESLZ?'" *AACJC Letter No. 204*. Washington, D.C.: American Association of Community and Junior Colleges, 1986.

Evans, G. "Social, Financial Barriers Blamed for Curbing Blacks' Access to College." *Chronicle of Higher Education*, August 7, 1985, pp. 1, 15.

Fleming, F. *Blacks in College: A Comparative Study of Students' Success in Black and in White Institutions*. San Francisco: Jossey-Bass, 1984.

Kalamazoo Valley Community College. *Minorities at Kalamazoo Valley Community College*. Kalamazoo, Mich.: Kalamazoo Valley Community College, 1988. 255 pp. (ED 293 586)

Michigan Department of Education. *Strategies for Recruitment and Retention of Minority Staff in Michigan Vocational Education Programs*. Lansing: Michigan Department of Education, 1986. 96 pp. (ED 263 343)

Mingle, J. R. *Focus on Minorities: Trends in Higher Education Participation and Success*. Denver, Colo.: Education Commission of the States and the State Higher Education Executive Officers, 1987. 50 pp. (ED 287 404)

Simpson, J. E. "Black College Students Are Viewed as Victims of Public Racism." *Wall Street Journal*, Apr. 3, 1987, pp. 1, 18.

Anne E. Mulder is president of Lake Michigan College, Benton Harbor, Michigan.

Connecticut's recognition of the need to respond decisively to the challenge of minority recruitment has led to a comprehensive array of programs to attract minority students.

Minority Student Recruitment: A Connecticut Model

Ronald A. Williams, Mary Anne Cox

In many respects the problems that colleges face today in attracting black and Hispanic students are the same that they have encountered for the past two decades. Colleges still face the challenge of integrating black and Hispanic students into the fabric of the educational and social mainstream. Education is caught in the spin of expectations, both social and industrial. In the last few years two interrelated events have occurred: one is the increasing popularity of the concept of educating the total work force; the other is the slowdown in the growth rate of the American population. Given the demographic shift that is taking place—that is, the slowdown of the birthrate among whites and the expected growth of black and Hispanic people as a percentage of the American population—we can expect that black and Hispanic people will drive America's future industrial development in an unprecedented fashion.

Against this background, which is as true in Connecticut as it is in the rest of the nation, a number of initiatives were developed to ensure increased minority participation in higher education. In the draft of the proposed recommendations of the Education Commission of the States National Task Force for Minority Achievement in Higher Education (1990, p. 1), the first recommendation notes, "College and university leaders can improve minority participation and achievement through effective leadership, appropriate policy goals, sound management practices and through reflecting in their own membership the cultural diversity of the populations they serve. Strategic planning should be used to define goals, collect data, allocate resources and establish measures to assess goal achievement. Goals

NEW DIRECTIONS FOR COMMUNITY COLLEGES, no. 74, Summer 1991 ©Jossey-Bass Inc., Publishers

should reflect the entire range of activities necessary for a systematic and coherent effort to increase both minority participation and achievement."

There appears to be a consensus that successful efforts to improve minority participation in higher education require a systematic approach proceeding from accepted policies to which the highest levels of institutional leadership subscribe. This is the approach which Connecticut has taken.

The Minority Enrollment Incentive Program

The Board of Governors for Higher Education, concerned about a downturn in minority college enrollments in Connecticut, created the Strategic Plan to Ensure Ethnic and Racial Diversity (1986). The plan's goal was to increase minority participation in Connecticut's colleges and universities by emphasizing minority recruitment and retention. In December 1986 the board of governors adopted the Minority Advancement Program, one component of which, the Minority Enrollment Incentive Program, will be discussed here.

The Minority Enrollment Incentive Program is intended to reduce by at least one-half the disparity between minority and nonminority enrollment and retention rates. Through the program the Department of Higher Education awards funds to public higher education institutions over a five-year period, based upon percentage improvements toward the achievement of the enrollment and retention goals. The total amount of incentive funding is fixed at $2.6 million. The total incentive payment during the five-year period takes into consideration the level of improvement necessary for the institution to reach its enrollment target, the institution's current level of black and Hispanic enrollment, and the total headcount enrollment of the institution. The actual payment is not on a per-student but on a percentage-improvement basis.

Minority incentive funds are used to offset counseling, admissions, and recruitment expenses; to provide remedial education or developmental programs; to pay for special programs for minority students in the college and at local public high schools; to provide student financial aid; and to cover indirect costs associated with the above. Each year, as part of the annual budget submission to the Board of Governors for Higher Education, each constituent unit must provide a report that describes actual award expenditures for each institution within its jurisdiction. According to the June 1989 Department of Higher Education report, Connecticut colleges and universities enrolled 18,644 minority students. This figure constituted 11 percent of the total student enrollment, the highest number and percentage in the state's history. Hispanic enrollment has increased almost by 30 percent and black enrollment by 17 percent since 1986.

Organization of Public Higher Education in Connecticut

In Connecticut public higher education is funded and controlled by the state. The Board of Governors for Higher Education has overall responsibility for the coordination of higher education policy for the state. Each constituent group of colleges—the University of Connecticut, the Connecticut State University, the Community and Technical Colleges, and the State Board for Academic Awards—has a board of trustees that governs the colleges under its jurisdiction. There are seventeen community and technical colleges, the presidents of which report to an executive director who reports to the Board of Trustees for Community-Technical Colleges.

Connecticut Community Colleges Long-Range Plan

The Board of Trustees for Community-Technical Colleges' approach to the challenge of recruiting and retaining minority students is comprehensive and inclusive. In 1988 the board adopted a long-range plan for the community colleges of Connecticut. The plan notes, "Central to our definition of excellence is our ability to provide services for all citizens of Connecticut. Our success must not be gained at the expense of access. . . . Clearly, if the Connecticut economy is to be adequately supplied with workers, the community colleges will be called upon to recruit, retain and graduate minority students in significant numbers" (Board of Trustees for Connecticut Community-Technical Colleges, 1988, p. 2). The long-range plan thus identifies a series of specific goals, with prescribed timelines and measures to achieve the larger objective of minority access. The programs described below constitute some of the initiatives undertaken by the plan.

Urban Marketing Initiative. The colleges recognize that it is not simply a case of providing prospective students with the information for choice among different institutions; rather, student interest must be awakened to the possibilities inherent in higher education. Recruitment is, therefore, a multifaceted campaign to make citizens aware of the community college and the college's creation of services and programs to respond to the multiple needs of the community's various populations. In order to accomplish this, a mass-media advertising campaign was initiated in spring 1988 to begin to increase the level of awareness about the colleges and their programs and to enhance the images of the colleges in the minority communities. Outdoor advertising began in 1988 and shifted in 1989 to transit ads in order to reach the urban population. One-minute radio commercials, using a testimonial format, were created, stressing the many benefits of college education to the minority audience. These were played on minority-oriented stations with statewide audiences. The other radio stations selected were those that also attract a large proportion of the minority audience. Half-minute television commercials using minorities were also developed; in addition to being aired on the three network-affiliated stations in Connecticut during their regular broadcast schedule, the commercials were also run during minority and/or public affairs programming. Minority newspapers and major metropolitan newspapers were also used in the recruitment campaign. Beyond this mass-media strategy, other publications aimed at minority high school students were targeted for recruitment advertising.

These centralized recruitment activities were supplemented by the colleges in their individual service regions. This marketing approach has been very useful in helping the community and technical colleges to enroll 66 percent of all the minority undergraduates in higher education in Connecticut. The marketing and advertising thrust attracted minority students to the following programs designed specifically with minority populations in mind.

The VIDA Program. At Greater Hartford Community College, the Hispanic Family Support program, known as VIDA, has been developed specifically to respond to the needs of Hispanic students in the Greater Hartford area. Aimed at a primarily female audience, VIDA is designed to provide education and support services to make economic self-sufficiency a reality for Hispanic women, many of whom are single heads of households facing difficulties in obtaining employment.

The VIDA program operates in three twelve-week cycles, beginning in September, January, and April, with approximately twenty participants in each cycle. Math skills, Spanish literacy, conversational English, and life-skills training are offered. A primary goal of the program is to identify barriers to employment and to help the participants overcome them. Beyond the basic education and career-oriented training, the participants with preschool children also have the opportunity to receive training in parenting skills from trained child-care specialists. Counseling in areas such as financial planning, health and nutrition, housing, and employment is also provided to the students.

Pre-Nursing Program. The Greater Hartford Community College also houses another notable program designed specifically to serve minority students. This is the Pre-Nursing program, which was developed in 1980 by the college's nursing department in order to increase minority participation in health care programs. A one-semester developmental program offered each spring, Pre-Nursing prepares approximately twenty students in each session for admission to the college's associate degree in nursing program. Four components comprise Pre-Nursing: communication skills, mathematics, science, and an introduction to nursing course. It is a full-time, fifteen-week, five-day-a-week, noncredit, pass/fail program that uses a diagnostic/prescriptive approach to teaching. The students learn to overcome cultural barriers, to improve decision-making skills, and to develop a regard for academic achievement through the strong counseling that is integrated into the curriculum.

Financial support is provided to each pre-nursing student during both the preliminary and the associate degree program. All course materials, uniforms, and physical examinations are furnished at no cost to the students, who in addition receive a stipend for living expenses. The program's budget also provides funding for financial emergencies and for additional nursing faculty to assist the students in both clinical and academic areas. Of the 108 students admitted to the program between 1980 and 1986, 98 students (91 percent) successfully completed Pre-Nursing and were admitted into the associate degree nursing program. Thirty-two of these students have graduated with the associate degree and are practicing registered nurses.

English-as-a-Second-Language Program. Several studies have noted that in the future new entrants into the work force will come from three groups—women, minorities, and immigrants. Many of the members of the immigrant groups will not have English as their first language; therefore, educational institutions will have to provide these students with the basic language skills they will need to function effectively in the work place. The English-as-a-Second-Language (ESL) initiative at Norwalk Community College is a response to another minority population, mainly Haitian and Puerto Rican, which has grown in its service region. The program has grown, along with its ethnic population, over the years, increasing from forty students in 1973 to more than seven hundred students during 1989-90. These students are served at both the college's main campus in Norwalk and its Language Center in Stamford.

Reading, writing, speaking, and listening to English are emphasized in all courses, with special emphasis placed on writing as the critical skill for future success. Each level, from basic to advanced (four in all), builds on skills developed at the previous level. Entrance into the program is based on a special test that assesses reading comprehension and grammar. Writing samples determine placement level and the advancement for each student. One hour of language lab instruction is required each week in each course, and tutoring services are available as well.

The English Skills Development Center, an integral part of the ESL program, provides an essential immersion component in language instruction by offering an increased number of classroom hours spent with an instructor during the first two levels. Small-group communication and interaction and tutorial services are also available through the Development Center. Comprehensive audio laboratories and computer-based instruction offer support in vocabulary, grammar, and usage exercises and help to reinforce material presented in the classroom. The center's enlarged ESL library of videotapes, publications, and computer programs also supports ESL and enriches each student's learning experience.

High School Partnerships Program. In June 1987 the board of trustees adopted a policy for a High School Partnerships Program. This policy recognized that colleges could provide high school students with more challenging educational experiences by expanding opportunities for them to attend accredited degree-granting institutions during their junior and senior years. The policy statement also noted that "in furtherance of the goal of expanded educational opportunity . . . [the program] is intended to go beyond traditional programs which concentrate primarily on serving gifted high school students. Rather, it is intended that the High School Partnerships Program be more expansive in providing an early experience to a more diverse group of high school students. . . ." (Board of Trustees for Connecticut Community-Technical Colleges, 1987). The program is operated under the following guidelines:

1. Each president enters into a written agreement with the superintendent of area school districts.
2. Commonly accepted admissions guidelines are established by the college and the school district.
3. The high school may offer concurrent or supplemental high school credit for courses taken at the college.
4. High school students admitted to the program will be eligible to enroll in a maximum of two college credit courses.
5. The college must make provision for academic advisement and other supportive services for the participants.
6. The college must attempt to schedule sufficient courses at times convenient for high school students to attend.
7. The college will pay the costs of tuition for the high school students participating in the program and will waive all fees.
8. The high school district and/or the student will be responsible for the cost of books and transportation. The college will encourage the school district to purchase the books.

South Central Community College in New Haven, Connecticut, has been particularly successful in attracting minority students using this program. Since the summer of 1987, the college entered into partnership agreements with school districts in its service region. During the fall of 1987, 142 students from eight high schools in four towns enrolled in thirty-four different courses. Almost 80 percent of the students were female (compared with the college's 70 percent female population), almost 46 percent were black (compared to 21 percent for the student body), and almost 8 percent were Hispanic (compared to 7.3 percent in the student body).

In the 1987–88 and the 1988–89 academic years, the community college system's High School Partnerships Program enrolled 608 students, of whom 438 successfully completed their course of study. To date, 53 students who participated in the program have enrolled as either full- or part-time students in the community colleges.

Minority Fellowship Program. As may be gleaned from the foregoing, the community and technical colleges of Connecticut have been very successful in attracting black and Hispanic students in large numbers. They currently enroll 662 of the state's undergraduate minority students.

The board of trustees recognizes that to serve these students well the colleges must provide role models for their students. In looking at the issue, the board of trustees quickly identified the need to attract more minority professionals into the colleges' staffs and faculties. Given the relatively small number of minority professionals available for positions, it was decided that if the college system was going to be successful in diversifying its work force, it would have to be more active in recruiting staff and faculty from minority groups and accept the responsibility for cultivating its own minority faculty. As part of the process of identifying and attracting minorities into the system, the board implemented the Minority Fellowship Program in 1988. This program is designed to identify minority graduate students who are at a minimum in the second year of a master's degree program, assign one to each college in the system, provide him or her with a mentor who is in the same academic discipline, and structure a significant teaching or administrative experience for each fellow. The fellow has to spend six to nine hours per week on campus and is involved in the regular activities of the campus, including attendance at departmental meetings and at professional development activities and orientations. The fellow also conducts a class under the supervision of the mentor. Each fellow is paid a stipend of $6,000 for the academic year, and the mentor is either awarded release time or undertakes the responsibility under the additional-duties clause in the contract. Because the colleges have the greatest need to diversify the faculty, only teaching fellowships have been authorized in the first three years of the fellowship program. Each fellow's application is reviewed by a screening committee that recommends the fellow to the president. The executive director has final approval. Two very interesting elements are worth noting about the program. It is jointly sponsored by the board of trustees and the professional staff and faculty union—the Congress of Connecticut Community Colleges—with the union providing $50,000 a year to support the program. Also, it has been agreed that a fellow can, at the discretion of the president, be offered a position in the college without a search if the following conditions applied: (1) a position and funds are available; (2) an affirmative action goal existed at the college for that category of employee; and (3) the fellow is given a satisfactory evaluation by the college.

The Minority Fellowship Program is in its second year, and recruitment is under way for the third year. In the two years the system has hired four full-time and three part-time faculty from this program, and it promises to continue to be a rich source of candidates for positions in the system.

Conclusion

The programs described above constitute a portion of the concerted activity in which the Community and Technical Colleges of Connecticut have been engaged in order to respond to the challenge of enrolling minority students in greater numbers. As many are beginning to realize and accept, finding solutions to the many social difficulties that minority students face is no longer merely a matter of humanitarianism but of national self-interest. Connecticut's planning and policy development and the activities of the system's seventeen colleges are designed to respond sensibly to this challenge.

References

Board of Trustees for Connecticut Community-Technical Colleges. *Policy Statement on High School Partnerships Program.* Hartford: Board of Trustees for Connecticut Community-Technical Colleges, 1987.

Board of Trustees for Connecticut Community-Technical Colleges. *Towards 2000: A Long-Range Plan for the Community Colleges of Connecticut.* Hartford: Board of Trustees for Connecticut Community-Technical Colleges, 1988. 61 pp. (ED 305 108)

Connecticut Department of Higher Education. *Strategic Plan to Ensure Ethnic and Racial Diversity.* Hartford: Connecticut Department of Higher Education, 1986.

Education Commission of the States. *Draft Report of the National Task Force for Minority Achievement in Higher Education.* Denver, Colo.: Education Commission of the States, 1990.

National Task Force for Minority Advancement in Higher Education. *Achieving Campus Diversity Policies for Change.* Denver, Colo.: Education Commission of the States, 1990.

Ronald A. Williams is assistant executive director of the Community-Technical College System of Connecticut.

Mary Anne Cox is director of marketing/public relations for the Community-Technical College System of Connecticut.

Although there have been numerous publications centered on the Hispanic and black student and a recent increase in articles concerning the Asian student, there is relatively little research focusing specifically on retention of the Native American student.

Minority Student Retention

James C. Henderson

The National Task Force for Minority Achievement in Higher Education, formed by the Education Commission of the States in June 1989, recommends that states establish "proportional enrollment and comparable achievement" as goals for higher education systems. The task force believes that every institution in a state is responsible for helping to ensure that minorities enroll in higher education in proportion to their representation in the college-going population and reach achievement levels in all fields of study comparable to nonminority students (Education Commission of the States, 1990).

The Native American Student

Although there have been numerous publications centered on the Hispanic and black student and a recent increase in articles concerning the Asian student, there is relatively little research focusing specifically on retention of the Native American student. A special report prepared by the Carnegie Foundation for the Advancement of Teaching (1989) presents perspectives on the tribal colleges located on the reservations that serve an entirely Indian student population. There are also community colleges outside of the reservation that have had marked success in serving the needs of the Native American student. The components that lead to success for the Native American student can also be applied to other minorities, but there are some unique factors relating specifically to the Native American that must be considered.

Educational Perspective. Native Americans are underrepresented in most institutions of higher education today. Because of the isolation of the

New Directions for Community Colleges, no. 74, Summer 1991   © Jossey-Bass Inc., Publishers

reservations, the cultural differences experienced between the two worlds occupied by Native Americans, and the expense involved in pursuing higher education, the barriers for young Indians seeking a degree are formidable. Very few colleges have sought out Native Americans. Their history in higher education has largely been one of exclusion or forced assimilation (Carnegie Foundation for the Advancement of Teaching, 1990).

American Indians have the highest dropout rate of all minorities. In the National Center for Education Statistics Dropout Rates in the United States report for 1988, the American Indians' dropout rate is 35.5 percent, compared to 22.2 percent for blacks, and 27.9 percent for Hispanics. The report also shows that Indians represent 3.1 percent of all dropouts, despite the fact that they account for only 0.9 percent of all elementary and secondary students (O'Brien, 1990).

Although American Indians are considered one minority group, in fact, there is wide diversity among the three hundred tribes in the continental United States and Alaska, and some two hundred languages are spoken. Awareness of the unique issues involved with Indian education is increasing, and both former Education Secretary Cavazos and Interior Secretary Lujan recently announced major initiatives to study and improve Indian education. Cavazos announced the establishment of a task force to review existing data and analyze all government programs that affect Indian education. Additionally, a series of meetings involving Bureau of Indian Affairs educators is currently taking place to discuss important Native American educational issues.

At many of the tribal colleges, retention remains a problem. For those who do finish school, the level of academic preparation is often very poor. The poor academic preparation and low self-esteem contribute to the dropout rate for Native Americans. Overall, at least 60 percent of white students who enter college obtain a degree, but less than one-third of the Indian college students graduate (Carnegie Foundation for the Advancement of Teaching, 1989).

The Community College Role. Community colleges across the nation are developing programs that address the needs of the increasingly diverse student population. The minority education initiative is the first priority listed in the mission statement of the American Association of Community and Junior Colleges (AACJC). "AACJC will assist colleges with the adoption of aggressive policies and practices to improve the recruitment, retention, and success of students, helping to guide minority students through a successful college experience" (AACJC Public Policy Agenda, 1990, p. 1). In *Building Communities: A Vision for the Future,* the community college is charged with the obligation to help students succeed in higher education. This is the central mandate of the report: "The community college must continue to offer all students an open door and reaffirm to minority students the promise of empowerment through education" (AACJC, 1989, p. 10).

As of 1988, over 93,000 Native Americans were enrolled at a variety of colleges, an increase of over 19 percent in just ten years, with the greatest growth (16 percent) occurring at two-year institutions (Evanlauf, 1988). Native Americans also earned 3,196 associate degrees from community colleges in 1986–87.

Yet for students who transfer to a four-year institution, a recent survey indicates that the matriculation rate is a mere 27 percent, with over half of the Indian students leaving at the end of their first year (Carnegie Foundation for the Advancement of Teaching, 1990). Nearly three out of four Native American college students fail to earn degrees because of poor academic preparation, inadequate financial aid, or personal problems (Wells, 1989). Moreover, though undergraduate enrollments are up, the number of Native Americans in professional schools has dropped by 22 percent. With the anticipated increase in Native Americans, enrollments in higher education will have to climb considerably merely to maintain the same proportion to tribal populations.

It will be the role of the community college to ensure that the Native Americans who enter these institutions are encouraged to remain in college to receive the academic, social, and individual support required for them to reach their full potential. The community college will be the institution that will increase the numbers of Native American students who successfully transfer to a four-year institution and obtain a degree.

Components for Success: San Juan College

Bridges to the Public Schools. In order to encourage minority students to begin thinking about college, bridges to the junior high schools and high schools have been built by New Mexico's San Juan College. The college operates an Area Vocational School for high school junior and senior students and has formulated two-plus-two articulation agreements with the four public school districts. Many minority students enter college with credits earned in high school that may be applied to certificate and degree programs. The high school–community college bridge is strengthened by high school counselors directing minority students to the two-year institutions. At the community college, minority students receive personalized instruction, tutoring services, and counseling, which assist in building academic success.

One of the most unique programs offered by San Juan College to assist its minority students is the Possible Dream Program. Most minority students at the college need financial assistance to achieve their educational goals. In addition to providing scholarships, grants, work-study opportunities, and loans, San Juan College has initiated a scholarship program for every eighth-grade student in the county. The college invites eighth-grade students to begin a $10-a-month, prepayment plan that will provide for two years of paid tuition when they are ready to enroll in the college. The program combines the monthly savings plan with a $125 scholarship, academic counseling, and a guarantee that tuition (now $360 annually) will not increase for those participating.

This program was designed to attract first-generation college students, many of whom are minorities. Now in its fourth year, the program is not limited to minority students, but 90 percent of the over four hundred students enrolled are members of a minority group. The Possible Dream Program builds an attitude among students in junior high school that college is within their reach. It motivates them to apply themselves while they are in high school so that they will be prepared to enter college. Family participation helps support the students' commitments.

In connection with the Possible Dream Program, the college has developed a matrix that identifies courses needed in high school to prepare for a specific college major. Each four-year institution within the region was canvassed for its specific major requirements, and the high school students are provided early information about the courses they need to reach their goals. The Possible Dream students are brought to the college campus for special orientation programs that encompass college offerings and career choices. A counselor works specifically with the Possible Dream students and their parents to encourage successful completion of high school and enrollment in college.

Native American Program. San Juan College retains a full-time director for the Native American Program who assists students in the transition from the reservation to college. The director provides counseling, assistance with scheduling, and information on tribal scholarships and financial aid.

Another function of the Native American Program is sponsorship of the Indian Club, the most active club on the San Juan College campus. The club provides leadership training for Native American students, as well as social interaction. Research indicates that students who are involved with campus organizations are more likely to complete a program than those who do not participate (Rooney, 1985). Being part of a group gives the students support, develops pride and confidence, and encourages them to be actively involved in college-wide activities. The club helps to foster the participation of many Native American students in other student organizations that focus on academic or vocational programs. These students successfully compete on state and national levels and serve as officers in the organizations. This involvement helps increase retention rates of minority students.

Assessment and Advisement. Critical to retention are assessment and advisement programs that place minority students in appropriate programs and at the correct level. San Juan College has established a placement testing center utilizing the computerized placement tests; these allow immediate scoring and generation of test results to aid college staff in placing students in suitable classes. The assessment results are organized and presented to the students in a manner that enables them to understand their readiness to do college-level academic work.

The assessment establishes the students' level in reading, writing, and math and their study skills. Upon completion of the assessment, students are assigned to a faculty adviser who helps develop a course of study suited to their abilities and goals. This faculty member also acts as a mentor for the student while he or she is enrolled at the college.

Renewal Center. If a student is experiencing difficulty in course work, tutoring is available at no cost. The Renewal Center also provides self-study materials, as well as specialized language programs, for students whose first language is not English. Additionally, the center operates Project Read, which teaches reading to Native Americans, including older adults—many of whom not only do not read in English but also may depend exclusively on spoken Navajo. The difficulties that Native American students often have with English are different from those experienced by native speakers of Spanish or other languages. For example, the Navajo language has no plural or tense, and English-as-a-Second-Language instruction provided to Native American students needs to reflect the basic differences.

Special workshops on financial aid, academic study skills, and basic tips for students returning to school are frequently held. Often some minor frustration that could have been corrected through better communication causes a student to leave the college. The Native American student tends to avoid conflict and may turn away from a problem rather than confront the issue or seek assistance in resolving it.

Outreach Programs. San Juan College has established a center located in close proximity to the reservation in which a variety of developmental, basic adult education, general education, and community service classes are offered. The director of the center is a Native American, as is the staff. The college also offers basic education classes in many locations on the reservation. Native Americans who may be too intimidated to come to the college campus feel more comfortable in a familiar setting. The attendance in these outreach programs has increased steadily and has led to students continuing their education at the college campus.

A unique program offered by the college is the Early Childhood Education Program, which offers college courses and individualized field training on site on the Jicarilla Apache and Navajo reservations. This program prepares candidates for the National Child Development Associate (CDA) credential. The college provides comprehensive training in a nontraditional, competency-based educational format. The training is provided to more than one hundred Native American Head Start teachers who have significant impact on the development of children living in geographically isolated areas of the reservation. Nearly 33 percent of the children in the county are Native American or Hispanic.

Building Success for Minority Students

Classroom Experiences. In a survey of San Juan College students, the Native Americans responded that one of the primary reasons for selecting San Juan College was the quality of education offered. The facilities and equipment available were also deciding factors. Students felt that they were being well prepared for employment or to transfer to a four-year institution. Other prime factors included low tuition and proximity to the reservation, although there is a branch of a tribal college close by.

Faculty Role. It is important to recognize that instruction in American college classrooms presumes certain Western cultural values. Student behaviors that instructors routinely reward and note as signs of student interest, effort, and intelligence are not necessarily behaviors that are rewarded in non-Western cultures. For example, many Native American students do not respond verbally in class, nor do they make direct eye contact, as both behaviors are considered impolite in their culture.

A diverse faculty is essential to a pluralistic campus. At San Juan College the Native American faculty members and staff are important to student retention. Quite often, it is these individuals who can help the Native American student gain the self-confidence required for academic success.

Beyond the Classroom. There are educational experiences that are especially beneficial to minority students that go beyond the textbook and the classroom. As previously mentioned, being actively involved in campus organizations and activities increases retention. Finding a peer group that is supportive, as well as faculty or staff members that can serve as mentors, gives the student the encouragement to remain and complete a degree.

Of great importance to minority students who have not had experience in the world of work is exposure to a business or industry setting. If a cooperative educational program is not available, two weeks of a semester spent in a work setting gives the student the opportunity to observe business practices before seeking employment. At San Juan College every student in the Business Education Program is assigned to a work station. The students set three goals to be completed during this period, and their assigned supervisor on the job evaluates their performance. For the minority students this may represent their first experience with real job practices. Human contact and personal development opportunities are also critical for success, especially among minority students, in dealing with other students and coworkers.

Empowerment. Students who succeed in the nation's community colleges and universities are those who feel committed to the pursuit of their education and who empower themselves to achieve by their demands for learning excellence. Minority students are no exception. Those students who are empowered possess several personal skills to achieve their goals. Among those skills are intellectual risk taking, culture-specific and cross-cultural interpersonal communication (ability to work effectively in the student's own culture and the mainstream culture), self-confidence, self-reliance, healthy physical and emotional self, problem-solving capability, and leadership abilities to work effectively within an organizational system (Terrell and Wright, 1988).

Through development of these and other empowerment skills, minority students can feel comfortable interacting in all campus situations. These skills are later transferable, so that students can then interact comfortably in the work place (Terrell and Wright, 1988).

Employment. Once the student has received an associate degree and has transferred or is employed, the effect of the retention effort can be measured. Through follow-up surveys of former students, a great deal of information can be obtained concerning reasons for choosing the institution and the factors influencing the decision to remain at the college to complete a program or a degree.

Native American students who attended San Juan College were recently surveyed to determine the factors that contributed to their continuing at the college. The students were employed at a major power plant and had successfully worked there for a number of years. The majority of respondents replied that the location close to home and low tuition were the major factors influencing their decision to attend the community college. Also of importance were the quality of the program and the interaction with the faculty. After graduating, the respondents felt they were well prepared to enter the work force. In reference to the preparation for employment, one respondent stated that more emphasis should be placed on problem-solving, decision-making, and creative skills in the courses.

The Human Resources Director at the power plant has developed a program to encourage the Native American employees to continue to learn, to establish goals, and to grow. She stated that the Native Americans have difficulty in setting goals and in thinking of future advancement. Through workshops the employees have developed more ability in these areas, which will lead to greater upward mobility. Retention programs for minority students in community colleges should consider these factors.

Transition to the University. Transfer from the community colleges to the four-year universities represents an important avenue to the baccalaureate degree in most states with large numbers of minority students (Richardson and Bender, 1987).

When a community college student has completed an associate degree and must repeat courses at the four-year institution, the student is penalized and discouraged from pursuing a baccalaureate degree. The citizens of the state are also penalized, for they have to pay twice for that student's education through state tax. Community colleges and four-year institutions must work together to increase the number of minorities transferring to senior institutions. Community colleges and senior institutions must also jointly develop and adhere to articulation agreements that facilitate transfer (Rendón and Taylor). However, there must also be serious commitment at the university level to create a climate that encourages minority student success.

Educating community college students to the changes that will be expected of them as they transfer to the university is essential. For the Native American student, this may be the first experience in a large urban setting. Bridge programs that offer university orientation at the community college level will help the student prepare for the transition. Moreover, the identification of mentors at the university to assist the transfer students before they leave the community college setting, during the transition period, and throughout the first year would improve the students' adjustment to a new environment.

States that have established articulation programs between the community colleges and the universities have increased transfer rates for minority students. Improving opportunities for minority student achievement requires institutional cooperation and the willingness to place state priorities for education above institutional interests (Richardson and Bender, 1987). As Parnell contends, "The Key is synergy. Different systems and different academic disciplines acting together with one accord to produce results greater than the sum of the parts" (Parnell, 1990, p. 225).

Conclusion

Through a mutual commitment by all educational institutions to increase minority student transfer, retention, and success, the numbers will grow. It is imperative that this commitment be instilled in the mission of each institution, for as minorities become the majority population their education may well affect the future of this nation.

References

American Association of Community and Junior Colleges. *Building Communities: A Vision for a New Century.* Washington, D.C.: American Association of Community and Junior Colleges, 1988. 58 pp. (ED 293 578)

American Association of Community and Junior Colleges. "1990 AACJC Public Policy Agenda." *Community, Technical, and Junior Colleges Journal,* 1990, *60* (4), 45–47.

Carnegie Foundation for the Advancement of Teaching. *Tribal Colleges: Shaping the Future of Native America. A Special Report.* Lawrenceville, N.J.: Carnegie Foundation for the Advancement of Teaching, 1989. 111 pp. (ED 311 990)

Carnegie Foundation for the Advancement of Teaching. "Native Americans and Higher Education: New Mood of Optimism." *Change,* 1990, *22* (1), 27–30.

Education Commission of the States. *Draft Report of the National Task Force for Minority Achievement in Higher Education.* Denver, Colo.: Education Commission of the States, 1990.

Evangelauf, J. "1988 Enrollments of All Racial Groups Hit Record Levels." *Chronicle of Higher Education,* April 11, 1990, pp. A1, A36–A46.

O'Brien, E. "The Demise of Native American Education." *Black Issues in Higher Education,* 1990, 7 (1) 15–20.

Parnell, D. *Dateline 2000: The New Higher Education Agenda.* Washington, D.C.: American Association of Community and Junior Colleges, 1990. 304 pp. (ED 316 270)

Rendón, L., and Taylor, M. "Hispanic Students: Action for Access." *Community, Technical, and Junior College Journal,* 1989–90, *60* (3), 19–23.

Richardson, R. C., Jr., and Bender, L. W. *Fostering Minority Access and Achievement in Higher Education: The Role of Urban Community Colleges and Universities.* San Francisco: Jossey-Bass, 1987. 244 pp. (ED 294 468)

Rooney, G. "Minority Students' Involvement in Minority Student Organizations: An Exploratory Study." *Journal of College Student Personnel,* 1985, *126* (5), 450–455.

Terrell, M. C., and Wright, D. J. *From Survival to Success.* Washington, D.C.: National Association of Student Personnel Administrators, 1988.

Wells, R. N., Jr. *The Forgotten Minority: Native Americans in Higher Education.* Canton, N.Y.: St. Lawrence University, 1989. 13 pp. (ED 317 346)

James Henderson is president of San Juan College in Farmington, New Mexico.

Effective retention programs must be designed to overcome minority attrition.

Minority Student Retention: The Prince George's Community College Program

David P. James

A number of community colleges and state boards have initiated retention programs and policy recommendations to deal with the problem of minority attrition.

Faculty and staff retention-mentoring programs have been shown to be positively related to minority persistence by the Illinois Community College Board (1989), Mendoza (1988), and Pulliams (1988).

The Jefferson Community College (1982) Recruitment, Retention and Attrition (RRA) program of 1978 has resulted in production of several pamphlets, including *Black Students—Special Problems/Special Needs for Retention,* designed to address the problem of black student attrition.

Background

During the past two decades, Prince George's Community College in Largo, Maryland, has experienced a dramatic increase in its minority student population, from only 9 percent in 1970, to the 54 percent current level. The enrollment of black students has increased from 552 in 1970 to 6,000 in 1989, representing 47 percent of the credit enrollment. Growing concerns with minority student performance prompted Prince George's Community College administrators to examine attrition patterns in the institution. Institutional data revealed consistently lower course-completion and retention rates for minority students, particularly blacks and Hispanics. Moreover, fewer than 16 percent of entering black students whose stated goal was to earn the associate in arts degree were doing so within a four-year period, an attainment level fully one-third less than that for white students.

Initial Retention Efforts

Between 1985 and 1987 the college developed a number of services intended to address student retention. These included a required system of assessment and advisement for newly enrolling degree-seeking students, tutoring in selected subject areas, and career assessment and planning programs. In addition, the Presidential Task Force was created in 1985 and charged with designing a comprehensive program for minority retention. In 1987 a collegewide committee was established to develop further retention efforts.

Yet despite these efforts, many black and minority students seemed to be unaware of these support services and did not participate in scheduled retention-related activities. In 1987 the task force proposed the College Success Project to increase the retention rate of first-time, full-time black male students. Black male students were targeted, based on the college's Office of Institutional Research and Analysis data on attrition, which clearly identified them as the students most at risk.

In 1987 the college received funding from the Maryland State Board of Higher Education to implement the College Success Program. Fifty first-time, full-time black males were selected for participation. Each student was assigned a mentor who assisted him in the development of college survival skills. Upon conclusion of the first year of grant funding, the Minority Advisory Committee was formed and recommended that the College Success Program be expanded to include first-time, full-time black females and renamed the Black Student Retention Program.

Present Institutional Models

Prince George's Community College secured state funding to implement the Black Student Retention Program. This funding proved to be a catalyst for a federal grant that enabled the college to develop a broad-based minority student retention program.

Objectives. The general objectives of the Black and Minority Student Retention Programs are (1) to increase the retention rate for first-time, full-time black male and female students, (2) to increase the retention rate for all other minority students (Asians, Hispanics, Native Americans), (3) to increase faculty and staff sensitivity and skills in working with minority student populations, (4) to improve minority student adaptation to the campus environment, and (5) to develop a comprehensive minority student retention program that is fully integrated within the college's organizational structure.

Support Services. The major supportive retention activities provided for both programs are the following:

- Mentors assigned to individual students
- Academic monitoring of all program participants during the third, fifth, and eighth weeks of the semester
- Career assessment and planning
- Personal-adjustment counseling
- Workshops and learning fairs focusing on college survival hints
- Tutorial services
- Parent/student/mentor orientation programs each semester
- Professional development activities to increase faculty and staff sensitivity and cross-cultural awareness
- Social and cultural activities promoting retention.

Selection Criteria for Students. Participation in the Black and Minority Student Retention Programs is voluntary. To be eligible for the support services provided by both programs, students are required to fill out an application. In addition, all applicants are required to sign the Mentee Agreement Form, which describes the responsibilities of student participants.

First-time, full-time black students are eligible for the Black Student Retention Program. All other minority students (Asians, Hispanics, Native Americans, and part-time black students) are eligible for the Minority Student Retention Program.

Mentoring. The major element of service for students in both programs is the individual support provided by mentors. All mentors are drawn from the college's full-time and part-time faculty, staff, and administrators. The mentors are selected by the project director based upon the following criteria: (1) successful record of working with students, (2) diverse backgrounds and interests, (3) professional training and experience, (4) academic and personal counseling skills, (5) knowledge of the college and its resources, and (6) desire to serve as a mentor (demonstrated by the application process). The mentor's responsibilities include monitoring participant academic progress, creating a supportive environment conducive to academic success, and initiating referrals to appropriate support-service units, such as the Writing Center, Tutoring Center, and Counseling Center.

Mentor-student matching is primarily based upon information listed on the student's application, including: (1) major or program of interest, (2) skills to be developed, (3) interest in student services such as tutoring, study skills counseling, and career assessment/planning, and (4) assistance needed to achieve personal and career goals.

All mentors participate in training workshops each semester. The workshops focus on effective techniques designed to assist mentors in developing positive relationships with minority students. Workshop training has also emphasized fostering supportive classroom environments for minority students and prescribing appropriate support-service referrals within the college. In August 1989 eighty-six mentors took part in a workshop as part of the college's fall professional development program. Participants rated this program as outstanding.

Students selected for program participation also receive direct instructional support from trained staff members of the college's Tutoring Center, Writing Center, Counseling (Career Assessment) Center, and Vocational Support Services. Instructional support personnel (including tutors) selected to participate in the retention programs undergo training similar to that provided for the mentors.

Results and Outcomes

Student participation in the Black Student Retention Program has increased from an initial enrollment of 34 in spring 1988 to 346 in fall 1989. Participation in the Minority Student Retention Program has grown from an initial enrollment of 92 students in spring 1989 to 221 in fall 1989.

The number of mentors providing individual support to program participants in both retention programs has increased from 11 in spring 1988 to 86 in fall 1989.

Black Student Retention. The spring 1988 to fall 1988 retention of Black Student Retention Program participants was 71 percent, twelve percentage points above the average retention rate for black students. Participant retention from fall 1988 to spring 1989 rose to 80 percent. From fall 1989 to spring 1990, participant retention rose to 83 percent, which exceeds the average rate for any identifiable student population subset on the campus.

Minority Student Retention. From spring 1989 to fall 1989 retention of Minority Student Retention Program participants was 67 percent, five percentage points above the average retention rate for minority students. Participant retention from fall 1989 to spring 1990 rose to 69 percent.

Orientation programs have been developed to provide structure to the relationship of mentors to participants and their parents. The orientation program, which was tested initially during August 1988, focuses on the nature of the mentoring relationship, the definition of academic and career goals, collegiate classroom expectations, orientation to campus support-service resources, and individual student problem-solving skills. Participants at the August 1988 to 1989 orientations numbered over three hundred and included student participants, parents, and faculty/staff mentors.

Program Assessment

The Office of Institutional Research and Analysis conducted an evaluation of the Black Student Retention Program during the spring 1989 semester to determine whether or not the program had an impact on the performance and retention of students who participated in the program during the fall 1988 semester. Outcomes were also calculated for two comparison groups: (1) first-time, full-time, degree-seeking black students who were not participants; (2) first-time, full-time, degree-seeking white students.

The highlights and findings of the report, *Assessment of the Black Student Retention Program: Program Evaluation PE89-1* (Prince George's Community College, 1989), were the following:

1. Sixty-six percent of the participants successfully completed 100 percent of their credit courses, equaling the percentage of the first-time, degree-seeking white group. In the black comparison group, only 51 percent completed 100 percent of their credit courses.

2. Eighty percent of the students who were mentees in fall 1988 returned to the college in spring 1989. Seventy-three percent of the black comparison group came back, and 83 percent of the white comparison group returned.

3. The average credit-hour completion rate of the groups were as follows: participant group, 81 percent; white comparison group, 81 percent; and black comparison group, 70 percent.

4. The average term grade-point average for each group was the following: participant Mentee group, 1.99; white comparison, 2.19; and black comparison, 1.58.

5. In addition, the report included the results of a survey of participants and mentors in the Black Student Retention Program. The findings were as follows:

(a) Ninety-one percent of the responding participants found the Black Student Retention Program helpful or very helpful;
(b) Ninety percent of the responding participants would recommend the program to a friend;
(c) Ninety-three percent of the responding mentors stated that their responsibilities were either clearly or very clearly defined;
(d) Eighty-eight percent of the responding mentors would like to continue as mentors.

In general, the indicators showed the participants performing on a level with or slightly below that of the first-time, full-time, degree-seeking white students. When compared with the black comparison group, the participants had a higher credit-hour completion rate, grade-point average, and fall-to-spring retention rate.

Conclusion

The implementation of the model Black and Minority Student Retention Programs has resulted in increased retention rates, decreased attrition rates, higher course-completion rates, expanded faculty/staff development programs for mentors, improved orientation programs for student participants and parents, positive student and mentor evaluations of the retention program, and the integration of the Black and Minority Student Retention Programs in the college's organizational structure through the administrative appointment of a project director.

Each institution needs to examine its institutional policies to determine their impact upon minority retention. Institutional commitment and the development of effective programs that appeal to large numbers of minority students can contribute to improved minority retention rates and, ultimately, increased graduation and transfer rates.

References

Illinois Community College Board. *Special Programs for Minority Students at Illinois Community Colleges.* Springfield: Illinois Community College Board, 1989. 12 pp. (ED 302 312)

Jefferson Community College. *Black Students—Special Problems/Special Needs for Retention.* Louisville, Ky.: Jefferson Community College, 1982. 5 pp. (ED 237 179)

Mendoza, J. *Developing and Implementing a Data Base and Microcomputer Tracking System to Track and Serve Minority Students to Enhance Minority Recruitment and Retention.* Glendale, Ariz.: Glendale Community College, 1988. 33 pp. (ED 301 292)

Prince George's Community College, Office of Institutional Research and Analysis. *Assessment of the Black Student Retention Program.* Program Evaluation, PE 89-1. Largo, Md.: Prince George's Community College, 1989.

Pulliams, P. "An Urban Community College Attempt to Assure Student Achievement: Creative Minority Initiatives." Paper presented at the 68th Annual Convention of the American Association of Community and Junior Colleges, Las Vegas, Nevada, Apr. 24-27, 1988. 21 pp. (ED 297 792)

David P. James is project director of the Black and Minority Student Retention Programs at Prince George's Community College, Largo, Maryland.

ENLACE has gained a national reputation for developing a model Hispanic community mentor program.

Minority Student Retention: ENLACE

Mauro Chavez, Margarita Maestas-Flores

The community college, which serves as a cost-effective system for entering higher education, must pay much closer attention to the impact of first-generation Hispanic college students and their underrepresentation in higher education. Retention studies reveal that in California, where the majority of postsecondary Hispanics attend community colleges, approximately 50 percent of these students drop out during their first semester. Several studies have examined low student self-esteem and low teacher expectations, noting that previous attempts at educational reforms for improved Hispanic participation in higher education have been unsuccessful because these conditions have remained unchanged. Unless alternative or nontraditional teaching and learning methodologies are adopted, Hispanics will continue to be blocked in their efforts to acquire a meaningful education. Further, educational programs that connect students with successful role models from the same ethnic background help develop in the students, teachers, and community a sense of what can be accomplished and leads to positive consequences (Cummins, 1986).

ENLACE

Enlace (en la ce), from the Spanish verb *enlazar,* means "to bind or connect," "to bring together," "to create community." The *enlace* concept is capable of producing an evolving network of educational and community professionals and can integrate knowledge, resources, and influence to effect change and result in educational success. Such a program exists at Evergreen Valley College (EVC). It serves educationally disadvantaged and underrepresented Hispanic students in San Jose, California.

A Shared Mission

Formerly the PUENTE Project at EVC, the program evolved from a statewide model into a comprehensive one that has created a more individualized campus and community-based approach to meeting EVC's student and local community needs. The faculty developed an all-Hispanic team consisting of an English instructor, a math instructor, a counselor, community mentors, a program/mentor coordinator, and an administrative supervisor. Three coordinating bodies were established to assist in the program's mission and goals: a college coordinating committee, a community mentor council, and a mentor math-advisory committee for the pilot math project. Hence, ENLACE, a program signifying "A Community's Investment in Education," was formalized at EVC in March 1989.

The faculty team at EVC understood that the success of Hispanics in the college's educational district would have to be based on the investment of the entire community. The team's task was thus to bind together teachers, counselors, administrators, students, mentors, community organizations, student organizations, and the corporate community.

The mission and goals defined by the ENLACE team involve the following measurable objectives:

1. To retain and matriculate Hispanic students in higher education
2. To enable Hispanic students to complete successfully the cognitive academic core (English and math)
3. To have Hispanic students effectively (and in a reasonable time) enter the general education/transfer/ occupational curricula
4. To enlarge the number of Hispanic students who graduate with an Associate in Arts or Associate in Science degree
5. To increase the number of Hispanic students who transfer to four-year colleges and universities.

The Cognitive Core. ENLACE emphasizes the successful completion of what is called the "cognitive core" areas of general/transfer education. As noted above, the core consists of English and math. ENLACE identifies the English and math disciplines as the "twin gates" of academic achievement because English (reading and writing) and mathematical skills lie at the heart of a student's academic success in the general/transfer education curricula. The English component at EVC consists of a two-semester course sequence, English 330/1A; and the math component is composed of a two-semester course sequence, Algebra I/II. Successful completion of the English 330/1A sequence prepares students to fulfill their social science and humanities requirements; Algebra I/II prepares students to fulfill their natural and physical science requirements within the general education curricula.

By developing a synergistic organization among team members, characterized by feelings of mutual trust, effective communication, role clarity, rapid feedback, and creativity, ENLACE provides students with individualized, nontraditional counseling, writing/math instruction, and personal contact with Hispanic professionals (mentors), who donate many hours in advising and assisting students to continue studies and pursue their educational goals.

Community Mentorship Program. ENLACE has gained a national reputation for developing a model Hispanic community mentor program. Lee Noel, president of the Center for Institutional Effectiveness and Innovations, referred to the EVC program as "one of the most progressive minority retention programs in the nation" (1988, p. 5).

The ENLACE Mentorship Program links Hispanic community professionals directly to the classroom learning process. For example, as part of their classroom assignments (particularly in English), ENLACE students work with a mentor whose profession is as closely related as possible to the student's major/career interest. The mentor activity is completed in addition to regular course requirements. The mentorship process has four objectives for the student:

1. *To Enhance Communication Skills.* Through the process of writing a letter of introduction, placing a telephone call to arrange an interview, and conducting an interview, the student utilizes communication skills. The requirement of preparing a mentor paper for the English class further improves writing abilities. Students develop drafts in class with their peers and share the final paper with the entire class—building oral communication skills, self-concept, and self-confidence. A final requirement of this assignment allows the student to write a letter of appreciation to the mentor.

2. *To Enhance Mathematical Skills.* Mentors from professions such as engineering, computer science, medicine, accounting, and business management are invited to the class to lecture on applied math (algebra), to explain how math relates to their professional area, and to participate in small group problem-solving sessions with students.

3. *Career Exposure.* As a result of interviewing a mentor, seeing the mentor on the job, and pursuing other contacts, students are exposed to a career field and have the opportunity to observe personally aspects of their career interest/educational major.

4. *Ethnic Identification in a Professional Field.* The mentor assignment allows students to see Hispanic role models; to share in a mentor's life, educational, cultural, and professional experiences; to see what it takes "to make it"; and to discover qualities the student may share with the mentor.

Although the mentorship assignment requires only the activities listed above, mentors and students are encouraged to continue contacts beyond the interview and classroom activities. Several long-term relationships have developed, some lasting through the student's studies at EVC and as he or she continues on to a four-year institution.

Results

ENLACE's model of linking classroom learning, counseling, and mentor experiences has proven highly successful. A three-year comparative study by the program's faculty of 115 ENLACE students and 273 non-ENLACE Hispanic students at EVC revealed several significant findings.

Students taught through the ENLACE model were almost twice as likely to complete English 330 than other Hispanic students enrolled in that course (89 percent/46 percent), completed English 1A at a rate nine times higher than their counterparts (70 percent/8 percent), completed English 1B at a rate fourteen times greater (14 percent/1 percent), and were three times as likely to be retained at EVC (53 percent/17 percent).

Whereas ENLACE participants accounted for only 30 percent of the total number of Hispanic students enrolled in English 330 during the three years, they accounted for 45 percent of the Hispanics who completed that course; 80 percent of the total who completed English 1A; 89 percent of those who finished English 1B; and 56 percent of the total number of Hispanics retained at EVC who began at the English 330 level.

ENLACE math students who enrolled in the Algebra I pilot section in fall 1988 completed the course at an 86 percent rate, compared to 36 percent for Hispanics in seven other college sections. Of that fall 1988 group, ENLACE students completed the spring 1989 Algebra II section at a 50 percent rate, compared to 2 percent for the general college group.

At the EVC Honors Convocation of May 1988, ENLACE students were represented in nine of the twenty-two college categories for scholarships/awards (41 percent). One ENLACE participant was the recipient of five scholarships—the most awarded in number or monetary amount to any one EVC student; this student was also the recipient of the Chicana Foundation Scholarship, one of three such northern California awards.

In 1989's All-College Honors Convocation, ENLACE students were represented in 42 percent of all categories, received 51 percent of all scholarship monies, and constituted 86 percent of all Hispanic students recognized for scholarships.

In a January 1989 statewide report identifying six other community college programs that focus on Hispanic student retention and transfer, EVC's ENLACE transferred twenty-one of fifty-one students reported since fall 1987—41 percent of the statewide total.

The data derived from the three-year study, the academic achievements of ENLACE students, and the current progress of students in the math pilot course have significance for the college and for the San Jose Hispanic community in the following areas:

1. The ENLACE instructional/counseling/mentor model improves the academic achievement levels of Hispanic students.

2. The structure serves to move more successfully "developmental English/ math" Hispanic students into the general education curricula.
3. ENLACE students have significantly higher retention levels than their non-ENLACE Hispanic counterparts at EVC.
4. The potential to transfer to four-year institutions, as well as that to complete requirements for the AA/AS degree, is significantly improved.
5. The model maximizes the opportunity for Hispanics to meet the matriculation goals of the college district.

References

Cummins, J. "Empowering Minority Students: A Framework for Intervention." *Harvard Educational Review*, 1986, *56* (1), 19–37.
Noel, L. "Cultural Attention to Student Retention," *Recruitment and Retention*, 1988, 2 (12), 8.

Mauro Chavez is associate provost, instructional services, and administrative supervisor, ENLACE, Evergreen Valley College, San Jose, California.

Margarita Maestas-Flores is program/mentor coordinator, ENLACE, Evergreen Valley College.

Several states have created public policy intended to perpetuate the ideals of educational equity.

Minority Transfer: A National and State Legislative Perspective

Louis W. Bender

A cynic might ask, "What kind of society is it that declares the highest of ideals in its nation's Constitution, yet responds more to economics or perceived crisis as the motivator of social progress than to its idealism?" It is a paradox that the truths like equality that guided the nation's founding fathers in drafting the Bill of Rights—and now found in charters and mission statements of both state and national public policy—are not found in the reality and daily activities of social institutions. This is true of higher education institutions, where deeds frequently fall short of, or are even contradictory to, the declaration of educational equity.

Our cynic could document the power of economics, as well as of real or perceived crisis, in obtaining institutional (and even individual) response. When the U.S. Court of Appeals in 1973 (*Adams v. Richardson*) upheld Judge John H. Pratt's order to dismantle ten previously segregated state higher education systems, a new agenda began to appear from state legislatures. To do otherwise would have resulted in loss of all federal funds, in effect an economic sanction against the state.

It took over a decade for all of the specified states to submit desegregation plans that were certified by the Office of Civil Rights of the Department of Education to be in compliance and thereby be removed from Judge Pratt's order to address imbalances of populations served.

Pratt's order in 1973 appears to have influenced a few states beyond those directly affected. Within a year of his order, the California legislature (in Assembly Concurrent Resolution 151) called upon the public higher education system to reach out to underrepresented groups and to ensure the system's students reflected the ethnic, gender, and economic composition of the state.

Several states have created public policy intended to perpetuate the ideals of educational equality. The Florida Equity Act of 1984 mandated: "Educational institutions within the state system of public education shall develop and implement methods and strategies to increase the participation of students of a particular race, national origin, sex, handicapped or marital status in programs and courses in which students of that particular race, national origin, sex, handicapped, or marital status have been traditionally underrepresented . . ." Illinois, New York, and Washington have comparable statutes.

Minority Transfer: A National Economic Issue

An optimist might predict significant progress on articulation/transfer issues and educational equity involving two-year and baccalaureate institutions over the next decade simply because economics is again rapidly emerging as the power source and motivator for action. The American citizenry, whether wealthy and influential or poor and disenfranchised, recognizes the challenge and danger implicit in competition within the contemporary and future global economy. When ours was an agrarian society, education was the appropriate and valued means to attain intellectualism and culture. Now the importance of all education to the nation's economic well-being has removed applied or practical education from the historic less worthy/less prestigious status and elevated it to the level of theoretical knowledge.

A concurrent evolution from the view of education as a privilege (pre-World War II) to education as a right has guided public policy. There is even a contemporary appreciation of the national need for each individual to be educated to his/her maximum capacity if our economic prominence in a global society is to be maintained. Regardless of socioeconomic status, race or ethnicity, gender, or handicapped or marital status, each individual is important to the economic health of the nation. It is inevitable, as Parnell (1990) predicts, that either our system of higher education will respond or society will create a new social institution that does.

The underrepresentation of ethnic minority groups among baccalaureate graduates has emerged as a national concern simply because the baccalaureate is the gateway to the professions. As studies have consistently shown that minorities are more likely to begin their postsecondary educational experience in a two-year college (Astin, 1985; Richardson and Bender, 1987; Wilson and Melendez, 1988), state legislatures are increasingly looking to articulation and transfer between two-year and four-year institutions as a vital link.

The perception of the public and its elected representatives is that transfer from two-year institutions to baccalaureate colleges and universities is a natural and free-flowing continuum. A central premise undergirding state systems of higher education as they have evolved during the era of open access is that students can freely move among institutions having significantly different missions, program emphases, and admissions criteria.

Studies of state coordinating-board policies too often fail to interpret or include institutional-level practice. The attitudes of faculty, relationships among key institutional administrators, and the magnitude of administrative bureaucracies influence the degree to which coordinating-board intentions become operational in the transfer experience. Furthermore, rarely are such studies disaggregated by race or ethnicity.

With nearly one-quarter of our land and resources now owned by other nations, the American public is looking for action from the national and state legislative policymakers. In turn, their policies are calling for higher education to deliver.

Problems of Legislation

A subtle but significant problem of legislation concerning ethnic-minority transfer students is the mislabeling by educators of certain legislative policies as minority initiatives. This practice can be verified easily by unobtrusively questioning administrators or faculty about the ethnic-minority-targeted services their institutions offer. Typically, among the answers will be assistance in overcoming academic deficiencies, financial aid policies, and advising and counseling practices (ranging from career, to academic, to "early alert" systems). In reality, such services are required by any student who arrives at the institution with deficiencies. Socioeconomic status is a better indicator that a student will need support than race or ethnicity.

A national longitudinal study of the activities and experiences of the 1980 class of high school seniors revealed that high socioeconomic status (SES) students were more than three times (61 percent) as likely to enter baccalaureate programs as were low-SES students (19 percent); low-SES students were also twice as likely to withdraw after entry as the high-SES entrants (National Center for Education Statistics, 1984). (SES was determined by the parents' education, family income, father's occupation, and household items.) Moreover, the participation rates of middle-SES students were consistently closer to the high SES group than the low SES group. Because minorities are disproportionately found to have lower SES, their transfer-program entry and success pattern mirrors their socioeconomic status and leads to the inaccurate generalization that academic support programs are minority initiatives.

Since the mid 1980s, the environmental factors that impede or serve as barriers to minority success have been identified by the American Council on Education, the Carnegie Foundation for the Advancement of Teaching, and researchers Allen (1986), Tinto (1987), Richardson and Bender (1987), and Boyer (1987). The educational environment, perceived or real, can be the determining factor in retention and success. Attitudinal factors, as well as behaviors, have increasingly emerged as critical elements of the campus and classroom atmosphere. Research has also consistently verified the central role faculty play in creating the environment and addressing the problems of transfer and articulation.

Existing Idealism

Our mythical cynic could point to an abundance of declarations from national and state leaders appealing to the idealism of institutions and faculties. For example, the Task Force on Minority Student Achievement of the State Higher Education Executive Officers (SHEEO) stated, "As educators, we can simply no longer content ourselves with the progress for minorities that is episodic, grudging and vulnerable to quick reversal at the slightest hint of benign indifference. What is needed is a level of commitment that produces change so fundamental that the risk of retreat is forever banished" (1987, p. 1).

The Ford Foundation has made a grant to the SHEEO organization to support a project to improve minority baccalaureate achievement through grants that will enable a number of states to strengthen collaboration, transfer policies, support mechanisms, and retention and to improve the campus environment, with the state coordinating agency playing a central role. The Ford and Mott Foundations, as well as several other philanthropic foundations, are increasingly directing resources to support minority transfer/articulation projects in response to an idealism that could result in substantive practices and change.

State master plans for higher education also establish priorities for institutions to achieve the ideal of educational equity and student success by translating words into deeds. Illinois, Maryland, New York, Florida, and California include provisions on minority-transfer success in their statewide master plans and periodically review the actual performance of the public institutions in achieving declared goals.

Even our cynic might become optimistic when observing the array of national organizations that have now established minority transfer as a national priority. The American Council on Education, supported by a Ford Foundation grant, has undertaken a project to foster educational equity with emphasis on transfer and articulation between two-year and four-year institutions. The American Association of Community and Junior Colleges adopted minority student success as one of its major public policy goals in 1990 and declared 1991 The Year of Transfer and Articulation. These national actions can contribute to awareness, open-mindedness, and commitment to action at the campus level.

Yet the key to success remains the human element on each campus, especially the faculty. Baccalaureate faculty are in a position to dictate the nature and level of cooperation, for they have ultimate authority over their curriculum. If they choose to remain in their ivory towers and be judgmental, articulation will not improve. But if they accept and respect two-year faculty as professionals and honor the integrity and appropriateness of their different institutional missions and cultures, then face-to-face faculty collaboration will assure minority student success.

A Policy Framework

Knoell (1990) and Bender (1990) agree that collaboration between two-year and four-year faculties represents the single most important element to be created if institutional response is to be positive and timely. Knoell advocates voluntary efforts, whereas Bender believes that legislative mandates are necessary in order to realize the necessary change in faculty attitudes and behaviors. Bender went so far as to advocate that Congress study the injustice to federal financial aid recipients and the cost to taxpayers that occurs when public institutions require such recipients to repeat course work that had already been successfully completed. Using the constitutional welfare-clause authority, Congress should enact legislation that would deny federal funds to states that do not correct such injustices.

Bender also recommended that Congress determine whether regional or professional accrediting bodies violate the rights of federal financial aid recipients when they impose requirements that are essentially barriers to transfer and articulation between two-year and four-year programs. Only one regional accrediting agency was identified in Bender's study as treating transfer and articulation in the same manner as affirmative action policies.

But the ultimate solution to the problem of education equity and minority transfer will emerge from each state's establishment of a policy framework for prioritization and action. Although individual states may have already enacted some or many of the provisions recommended below, none have provided for a comprehensive, systematic framework.

First, the legislature, governor, and higher education boards (whether coordinating or governing and representing each sector or all sectors of the postsecondary system) must make a commitment to policies and programs that insure an educational environment of fairness and responsiveness for each student, regardless of race, ethnicity, gender, or economic circumstance.

Second, an independent task force representative of each state's ethnic composition should be established to determine at both state and campus levels the status of educational equity and minority-transfer success.

Third, each public institution should be required to develop campus policies that foster an appreciation of all individuals, regardless of heritage and background, and that include provisions for preventing, reporting, monitoring, evaluating, and responding to acts of prejudice, hatred, and violence.

Fourth, the legislature should provide incentive programs to financially support or reward institutions that cooperatively conduct early outreach programs, summer bridge programs, and dual-enrollment programs focused on underrepresented minority-student populations. Furthermore, legislatures should provide incentive differential funding for upper-division institutions that formalize recruitment, admissions, orientation, and other support of minority associate-degree-graduate transfers. Research has conclusively verified the significant enhancement for completion and grade-point-average success when students complete associate degree requirements before transferring.

Fifth, legislatures should offer incentive funding for initiatives designed to increase minority enrollment in fields where minorities are underrepresented. Two-year and four-year institutions should also be rewarded when they establish goals and measurable objectives to increase the number of minority students who transfer.

Sixth, legislatures must also provide special funding or incentive grants for programs promoting sensitivity training for college professional and support personnel on issues of race, class, and culture. Faculty senates or comparable faculty governance bodies should be called upon to establish policies and programs that support multicultural understanding and educational equity.

Seventh, every state needs an information system with data bases that furnish a clear picture of transfer activity, including facts about the flow of transfer and a record of student progress after transfer. The information system should also assess the effectiveness of transfer policies and procedures by identifying the problems encountered by minority students when transferring, as well as other barriers that inhibit minority transfer.

Eighth, the information system should be comprehensive and support the transfer process by including computerized course-equivalency information, course prerequisite/requisite requirements for majors, and electronic transcripts.

Finally, legislatures should require a biannual report on progress and problems in achieving true education equity from both the coordinating or governing boards of the institutions, as well as from the task force on educational equity.

References

Allen, W. *Campus, Gender, Race Differences in Black Students' Academic Performance, Racial Attitudes and College Satisfaction*. Atlanta, Ga.: Southern Education Foundation, 1986. 123 pp. (ED 268 855)

Astin, A. W. *Achieving Educational Excellence: A Critical Assessment of Priorities and Practices in Higher Education*. San Francisco: Jossey-Bass, 1985.

Bender, L. W. *Spotlight on the Transfer Function: A National Study of State Policies and Practices.* Washington, D.C.: American Association of Community and Junior Colleges, 1990. 78 pp. (ED 317 246)

Boyer, E. *College: The Undergraduate Experience in America.* New York: Harper & Row, 1987.

Jaschik, S. "State Leaders Urged to Intensify Colleges' Efforts to Enroll and Graduate More Minority Students." *Chronicle of Higher Education,* July 15, 1987, pp. 1, 22.

Knoell, D. M. *Transfer, Articulation, and Collaboration: Twenty-Five Years Later: A Restudy of Relationships Between Two- and Four-Year Institutions.* Washington, D.C.: American Association of Community and Junior Colleges, 1990. 109 pp. (ED 318 528)

National Center for Education Statistics. *The Condition of Education: A Statistical Profile.* Washington, D.C.: U.S. Department of Education, 1984. 231 pp. (ED 246 521)

Parnell, D. *Dateline 2000: The New Higher Education Agenda.* Washington, D.C.: American Association of Community and Junior Colleges, 1990. 304 pp. (ED 316 270)

Richardson, R. C., Jr., and Bender, L. W. *Fostering Minority Access and Achievement in Higher Education: The Role of Urban Community Colleges and Universities.* San Francisco: Jossey-Bass, 1987.

Tinto, V. *Leaving College: Rethinking the Causes and Cures of Student Attrition.* Chicago: University of Chicago Press, 1987.

Wilson, R., and Melendez, S. E. *Minorities in Higher Education: Seventh Annual Status Report.* Washington, D.C.: American Council on Education, 1988.

Louis W. Bender is professor of Higher Education and director of the State and Regional Higher Education Center at the Florida State University, Tallahassee.

We need to focus on transfer as an activity that students undertake, not simply as institutional actions to assist transfer students.

The Many Faces of Transfer Education

Judith S. Eaton

When faculty and administrators at various community colleges begin to talk about transfer, it quickly becomes apparent that they mean a variety of quite different institutional functions. *Transfer,* for the purposes of this chapter, refers to a particular form of behavior in which students seek to move from a two-year school to a four-year institution. Yet if we visited any number of community colleges throughout the country, we also would find transfer identified with articulation agreements, the liberal arts curriculum, a counseling and advising center, or institutional research efforts.

When we talk about transfer in terms of diverse institutional operations, what we mean is less than clear. This circumstance contributes to a further confusion in our thinking in that we treat transfer as something colleges do as distinct from something that students do. If we seek to define a desired institutional role and to identify transfer success and failure, we need to focus on transfer as an activity that students undertake, not simply as activities by institutions to assist transfer students.

The transfer function, in the minds of some, is not a matter for individual institutions alone. Transfer involves the relationship between and among different kinds of institutions and, as such, calls for forms of control and management that supersede the authority of any single college. Transfer issues are then described in the language of course-equivalency guides, through pages in college catalogues, and other written agreements, perhaps for regions or consortia. At times, this approach involves bilateral or multilateral institutional arrangements. In other instances, it involves state-elected officials, state bureaucracy, or state agencies. It may concern interested constituencies or various interest groups, such as community-based organizations or those concerned with the implications of transfer for

NEW DIRECTIONS FOR COMMUNITY COLLEGES, no. 74, Summer 1991 ©Jossey-Bass Inc., Publishers

women and minorities. At yet other times, institutional commitment to transfer is affected by the prevailing policy position of national organizations. To the extent that community colleges allow themselves to be led by the policy preferences and values of those outside their institutions or even geographic areas, they are failing to meet an institutional responsibility and important educational obligation.

When we begin to probe the phenomenon of transfer, we find ourselves dealing with a surprisingly complex academic and political issue, going well beyond the apparently common-sense notion with which we are familiar. Examining transfer reveals touchy political dimensions within an institution, arising from faculty involvement, academic preferences, and the politics of the curriculum. Additionally, the transfer function is viewed as problematic with community college educators who are sometimes uncertain of how it fits within the polymorphous mission of their institutions. Finally, effective transfer involves grappling with difficult academic and organizational decisions, such as the question of sanctioning early transfer, the support of career transfer, developmental education and transfer, and equity issues.

Underlying the various approaches on the part of community college educators to transfer—whether discussed in terms of regulation, contribution to baccalaureate education, or, as will be further discussed, data and definition—are broad and emotionally charged issues of community college mission and purpose. Those who view community colleges as comprehensive value the transfer function, but not too much. Educators who see the efforts of community colleges as primarily directed to vocational students are apprehensive about the current emphasis on transfer. Some are even threatened; they perceive community colleges as being urged to return to a junior-college status and to renounce a successful vocational emphasis. Finally (and for reasons not at all clear), when transfer is probed as a measure of institutional effectiveness, it is viewed as a challenge to fundamental community college worth in a way that similar scrutiny of, for example, occupational education enrollments would not be. Perhaps the reason is that transfer education is the primary means whereby community colleges assert themselves academically within higher education. Perhaps transfer education is viewed as collegiate in a way that occupational and developmental education are not. Perhaps the reason is related to an anti-intellectualism that is reflected in the thinking of many community college practitioners.

This chapter examines the complexities of transfer education in community colleges today. Although we acknowledge that there are important issues in transfer education involving four-year schools, the role of these institutions is not discussed. Rather, the chapter focuses on various treatments of transfer education in community colleges: transfer as defined by student behavior, transfer as described by institutional or organizational behavior, and transfer as described by academic practices. It ends with a recommendation that we pay especially close attention to academic practices and an academic model of transfer education as a particularly valuable conceptual approach to the improvement of transfer education in community colleges.

Transfer as a Matter of Student Behavior

In 1989 and 1990 we saw a number of reports and books issued that focused attention on the transfer function of community colleges. Their analysis of transfer activity was based on quantitative descriptions of student behavior. For the most part, these works were based on two data sets, the National Longitudinal Study (NLS) of 1972 high school graduates and the High School and Beyond (HSB) data collected on high school graduates beginning in 1980, as well as on work done in various states such as New York and California.

Although there was virtually no agreement about a definition of transfer, critics such as Pincus and Archer (1989), Brint and Karabel (1989), Lee and Frank (1989), and Dougherty (1987) found community colleges to be relatively ineffective agents of educational, and thus socioeconomic, mobility. Their observations were grounded in two concerns: the limited extent to which community colleges were assisting students, especially minority students, to move into baccalaureate institutions and, as a consequence, the limited extent to which community colleges were effective catalysts in the redressing of social inequality.

Observers who were less disparaging of community college efforts, such as Grubb (1990), Adelman (1989), and Cohen and Brawer (1989), differed from the critics not so much in the quantitative descriptions of transfer activity but in their judgments about whether these descriptions reflected effective or ineffective transfer commitment on the part of community colleges. They did not rush to judgment about community college transfer success or the lack thereof. Transfer rates, as described by critics and observers alike, ranged from 5 percent to 30 percent of the community college student population, depending on the source and the definition of transfer.

The analysis of the NLS 1972 data base by Adelman (1989) provides significant information on transfer education in community colleges. NLS has several advantages: it is based on transcripts as well as surveys; it provides a sixteen-year profile of students' education (as compared with information generated about community college students only four or six years after their high school graduation); and it can be compared to surveys of student self-reporting about their educational activity in order to confirm the accuracy of these surveys. It also has some disadvantages: the transcripts are for only 12,600 students; substantive judgments have to be made about the meaning of some inconclusive transcript data; and the relationship between the transcript data and the survey data is not always clear.

Nonetheless, as Adelman indicates, NLS data tell us a good deal about the transfer behavior of the 1972 group. The data indicate that one in seven students in the NLS attended a community college. Approximately nine percent (8.9 percent) of 1972 high school graduates who entered postsecondary education attended a community college and went on to earn a baccalaureate degree. Half of this nine percent earned an associate degree as well. Six percent of the students in the NLS attended both a community college and a four-year institution, with one-third of them earning an associate degree but not the baccalaureate.

Adelman's analysis confirms that transfer from and degree acquisition in community colleges are limited activities for the NLS 1972 population. He further maintains that community colleges function as occasional or intermediary or testing-ground institutions; that community colleges serve curricular purposes in the areas of health, business, engineering, and general studies more readily than the traditional liberal arts; and that community colleges will continue to serve majority students in significantly greater numbers than minority students.

Pincus and Archer, relying on work by Cohen and Brawer, Bensimon, and Palmer, suggest that community college transfer activity is limited to 15 to 25 percent of the general student population and to 20 to 30 percent of those who state an intent to transfer. Lee and Frank, using High School and Beyond data four years out, puts the transfer rate at 24.3 percent. Although Pincus and Archer and Lee and Frank do not establish benchmarks of transfer success on either an institutional, state, or national basis, they do conclude that the community college transfer experience involves too few people, especially (according to Pincus and Archer) too few blacks and Hispanics. Grubb compares transfer and baccalaureate attainment for those in the NLS study and the HSB studies four years out of high school and concludes that transfer activity in community colleges, as measured by either associate degree acquisition, baccalaureate degree acquisition, or transfer without a degree, is declining. Brint and Karabel conclude that the limited transfer activity of the community college is essentially a product of the ethos of vocationalism, an ethos that they contend was forced on community college faculty and students by national community college leadership.

Studies of transfer rates are largely confined to a few sophisticated community college states such as Florida, Illinois, Texas, and California. Here, the absence in many cases of any consistently applied definition of transfer, as well as pressure to meet the concerns and criticisms of legislators and education policymakers, results in uneven and inconclusive state reporting. The absence of institutional capacity to collect longitudinal data on transfer students and the institutional failure to define transfer consistently are in part responsible for this situation.

At least two national efforts are under way to define transfer and develop data by the Center for the Study of Community Colleges (CSCC) and the National Effectiveness Transfer Consortium (NETC). Both focus on first defining transfer and then establishing institutional transfer rates. To date, CSCC has worked with forty-eight institutions and NETC with twenty-eight colleges. The American Association of Community and Junior Colleges is not engaged in any major study of transfer activity at this time but has urged that the transfer issue be framed less in terms of rates and more in terms of student intention to transfer and of the extent to which community college education was part of the prior education experience of baccalaureate-degree holders.

Transfer as described by student behavior, then, involves a variety of definitions and descriptions of numbers of students transferring. To understand the effectiveness of the transfer function, what counts as transfer success, and the strength of transfer education in community colleges based on analysis of student behavior, we will at some point need to arrive at some agreement about the manner in which we quantitatively describe transfer activity in our institutions.

Transfer as a Matter of Regulation of Organizational Behavior

Some observers do not focus on the extensiveness of transfer activity but on the governing relationships associated with transfer. Knoell (1990), Kintzer (1989), and Bender (1990) all concentrate their efforts on articulation agreements, laws, or regulations associated with transfer. They do not approach the issue from a quantitative perspective, or by attempts to define transfer, or by use of student transfer traffic as a basis for determining transfer success or failure. As a group, these researchers' underlying assumption appears to be that if we have effective agreements about elements of transfer (such as course-equivalency guides, registration, and honoring of the associate degree), we can consider our institutional effort successful without having to count transfer students.

The notion here is that such arrangements make transfer possible for whoever is interested and that we should not have preconceptions regarding transfer success defined by an arbitrary rate. This group of observers places considerable confidence in the impact of state regulation. Those pursuing this approach to transfer education distinguish among law, guideline, and regulation used at the state level to govern transfer. Kintzer identifies thirty states involved in monitoring transfer through at least one of these strategies. Bender points out that the designation *community college* covers a multitude of kinds of two-year institutions and that any evaluation of the nature of state control must be considered in light of this fact. Bender also urges that we focus on institutional leadership, faculty involvement, and the role of accrediting bodies in order to improve transfer. He suggests that there be federal- and state-level scrutiny of student and institutional assistance programs in order to avoid duplication of financial assistance, that federal and state governments influence accrediting agencies to ensure that barriers to transfer do not exist, and that transfer and articulation become major agenda items for the American Association of Community and Junior Colleges.

Knoell's major study of the past twenty-five years of transfer and articulation, funded by the Ford Foundation, is global; it makes recommendations for government, institutions, and faculty, aimed at further structuring transfer activity. Knoell appears uncomfortable with linking transfer success to transfer rates. She looks to the strengthening of transfer through increasingly careful governing of key elements of transfer relationships, such as student flow, the policy preferences of elected officials, admissions practices, and systemwide regulations. The works of Knoell, Bender, and Kintzer do not address the evidence about whether government interventions make a difference: there are states in which there are articulation agreements and evidence of significant transfer activity and also states with fairly elaborate articulation structures and limited transfer activity. Abundant transfer activity is not always accompanied by state regulatory behavior.

Transfer as a Matter of Academic Practice

The traditional academic approach to transfer involves assuring that full-time associate-degree seekers match their two-year program with a baccalaureate program. This practice can work well when there are some shared understandings about course content and academic standards. This cooperation is most likely to occur when a community college has been able to sustain strong college-level academic programs for reasonably well-prepared students. When community colleges have populations of significantly underprepared students who are working, who are part-time to the point where they have no recognizable program, or who are in nondegree programs, transfer is problematic.

Transfer education poses additional academic challenges. Most community college students who transfer do so early, prior to earning an associate degree. Yet we have not organized and structured the transfer experience for these people. Some states like California or Texas emphasize transfer independent of earning a degree, thereby rendering associate-degree status as essentially irrelevant to the baccalaureate.

Transfer education is generally identified with liberal arts or general education students in community colleges. However, there are significant numbers of career-education students in community colleges who transfer.

Transfer education in many community colleges is not adequately connected to developmental programs so that remedial students can focus on longer-range educational goals. Finally, transfer education is still predominantly described as if students attended school full-time. There are few models for part-time, working, community college students who still wish to structure a transfer education.

The National Center for Academic Achievement and Transfer, funded by the Ford Foundation and the American Council on Education, is attempting to strengthen transfer education in community colleges, especially for black, Hispanic, and disadvantaged students, using primarily an emphasis on academic practices accompanied by evaluation of transfer effectiveness based on quantitative analysis of student behavior. It stresses an academic model in its approach. The National Transfer Center is engaged in several major activities, including a national Partnership Grant Program in which approximately $2,000,000 will be invested in bringing two- and four-year institutions together to redesign curricula, address issues of academic standards, and scrutinize pedagogy. In that it builds upon an academic model of effectiveness, the National Transfer Center differs from other major efforts to improve transfer through articulation or student service programs. An academic model is founded on the idea that dealing with teaching and learning issues is central to effectiveness, as indicated either by students transferring in numbers considered to indicate success or by the ease with which students in whatever numbers are able to successfully navigate interinstitutional transfer waterways. Faculty agreement about course content and expected performance of students is essential to the academic model as well.

An academic model of successful transfer calls for institutional examination of the courses and programs students use for transfer purposes, whether full- or part-time, degree or nondegree. The model requires consideration of the fit—in content and in requirements—between this community college course work and the four-year curriculum. It stresses that faculty at two- and four-year institutions work together to ensure that curricular substance and expectations regarding students' skills are consistent; and, therefore, that students are able, upon transfer, to handle successfully baccalaureate work. The academic model goes beyond the premise characteristic of articulation efforts that courses or programs already in existence will complement one another, to the actual collaborative development of curriculum content and academic performance. It places primary emphasis on the building of curriculum used for transfer as a shared enterprise between two institutions and as a fundamental mechanism to assure that community college students engage in learning activities that will be of greatest benefit in a four-year setting.

The critical point is the emphasis on shared curriculum and pedagogical development, as distinct from an approach where faculty try to cooperate after teaching and learning decisions have been made at their respective institutions. The academic model urges collaboration in the development of the transfer experience as distinct from reconciliation of already established and different transfer expectations at two- and four-year institutions.

The academic model is not an easy approach. It must take into account the politics of the curriculum, both within and among institutions. It forces us to confront differences of opinion about important academic issues such as general education, liberal arts distribution requirements, and institutional performance standards. It calls for cooperation concerning curriculum that is extraordinarily difficult to achieve in even one college or university, compounded by the need to bring two institutions together. The academic model also suggests that meaningful change takes place neither easily nor quickly: the politics of curriculum development result in a pace of change that is slow and deliberate, reflective of the inertial character of department and faculty politics.

The academic model moves us immediately into the difficult arena of varying approaches to academic standards, alternative visions of an educated person, varying ideas about curricular content, and sincere differences of opinion regarding access and achievement in higher education. The academic model involves confronting the most fundamental intellectual values of the community college.

In summary, an academic model for transfer education is built upon two obvious yet powerful assumptions about academic life: the greatest amount of a student's time on campus is spent with faculty in the classroom, and institutional expectations about transfer are based on academic decisions about course substance and academic standards. Students who transfer do so on the basis of agreements about academic content and standards. The academic model stresses the collaborative development of responses to critical questions of course substance, desired pedagogy, and academic standards as distinct from unilateral development of courses and standards within individual institutions to be followed by efforts to find areas of agreement with other institutions. The academic model focuses on the academic competence and capacity needed by students for baccalaureate-level work, stresses the creation of shared understandings and expectations between the academic faculty and administrators at two- and four-year institutions, and emphasizes agreement about curriculum content and levels of academic performance.

The academic model is enhanced by attention to student behavior as a means of identifying the extent of transfer activity and establishing benchmarks of transfer success. Here the Cohen and Brawer definition of a transfer rate, emerging from the Ford Foundation–funded Transfer Assembly, is especially valuable. Cohen and Brawer call for establishing a transfer rate based upon institutional data on community college students who are followed longitudinally through their respective academic careers. Cohen and Brawer define transfer rate from analysis of that population of students (1) with no prior college experience, (2) who have completed at least twelve college credits in the community college, and (3) who, within five years of entering the community college, took at least one credit course at a four-year school. The forty-eight institutions with which they have worked using this definition identified a transfer rate of 23 percent. The institutions willing to undertake this approach to transfer have a twofold task: to establish a research program to ensure longitudinal data collection and, based on their information on transfer rates, to establish benchmarks of institutional transfer success or failure. It is one thing to have information concerning an institutional transfer rate; it is another to identify indicators of effectiveness based on careful consideration of institutional purpose and context.

Conclusion

The transfer function in community colleges to date has taken on many forms and is guided by a decidedly diverse set of assumptions about the purpose of community college education. It is unlikely that any one view of transfer education will prevail. What is probable is that we will see increased concentration of attention on the various transfer issues with a twofold result: we will do a better job of describing and analyzing transfer activity within our institutions as measured by the numbers of students transferring, and transfer students' success in attaining the baccalaureate will increase. The transfer function of the community college—its skill at assisting and enabling students to move successfully into four-year institutions—will emerge enriched and strengthened.

References

Adelman, C. "Using Transcripts to Validate Institutional Mission: The Role of the Community College in the Postsecondary Experience of a Generation." Paper presented at the annual meeting of the Association for the Study of Higher Education, Atlanta, Ga., Nov. 2-5, 1989. 59 pp. (ED 313 963)

Bender, L. W. Spotlight on the Transfer Function: A National Study of State Policies and Practices. Washington, D.C.: American Association of Community and Junior Colleges, 1990. 78 pp. (ED 317 246)

Brint, S., and Karabel, J., The Diverted Dream: Community Colleges and the Promise of Educational Opportunity in America, 1900–1985. New York: Oxford University Press, 1989.

Cohen, A. M., and Brawer, F. B. The American Community College. (2nd ed.) San Francisco: Jossey-Bass, 1989. 485 pp. (ED 309 828)

Dougherty, K. "The Effects of Community Colleges: Aid or Hindrance to Socioeconomic Attainment?" Sociology of Education, 1987, 60, 86–103.

Grubb, W. N. *The Decline of Community College Transfer Rates: Evidence from National Longitudinal Surveys.* Berkeley, Calif.: Institute for the Study of Family, Work, and Community, 1990. 41 pp. (ED 315 125)

Kintzer, F. C. *Articulation and Transfer: A Review of Current Literature on Statewide Programs and Interinstitutional Program Models and Trends.* Trenton: New Jersey State Department of Education, Office of Research, 1989. 71 pp. (ED 311 946)

Knoell, D. M. *Transfer, Articulation, and Collaboration Twenty-Five Years Later: A Restudy of Relationships Between Two- and Four-Year Institutions.* Washington, D.C.: American Association of Community and Junior Colleges, 1990. 109 pp. (ED 318 528)

Lee, V., and Frank, K. *Student Characteristics Which Facilitate Transfer from 2-Year to 4-Year Colleges.* Ann Arbor: University of Michigan, 1989. 35 pp. (ED 315 124)

Pincus, F., and Archer, E. *Bridges to Opportunity: Are Community Colleges Meeting the Transfer Needs of Minority Students?* Washington, D.C.: Academy for Educational Development, 1989. 60 pp. (ED 312 026)

Judith Eaton is vice-president of the American Council on Education and director of the National Center for Academic Achievement and Transfer, Washington, D.C.

Community colleges trying to strengthen the transfer function must not ignore the central importance of curriculum for empowering minority students to achieve educational goals.

A Model in Community College Transfer Programs

Aram L. Terzian

Strengthening the transfer function of community colleges centers on two fundamental and closely related tasks. The first of these is the responsibility to provide a coherent and appropriate educational experience for students. Richardson, Fisk, and Okun (1983) identified the lowering of literacy norms in the community college classroom and student failure to pursue a coherent program of study as major impediments to the upward mobility of community college students. Cohen and Brawer (1987) have been concerned that colleges surrender their authority over the scope and direction of student learning in the liberal arts when they promote and certify indiscriminate student course taking. They have perceived recent curriculum efforts in community colleges as moving towards effective sequencing and program completion, academic acculturation, and a renewed interest in social justice.

The second task for strengthening transfer is providing a supportive academic environment that encourages and motivates students to take themselves seriously as learners. This task can be accomplished by developing a special kind of academic community around the curriculum that provides the support and encouragement students need, both to see transfer as an option and to successfully move on to four-year colleges. Rendón and Nora (1988) pointed to a variety of student and institutional attitudes that weaken the possibility of minority students transferring to four-year colleges. Their interpretation of studies of student behavior suggests that although most students plan to transfer, they are not integrated in the social community of the college, are not encouraged to seek transfer as an option, and have few contacts with faculty outside of the classroom.

NEW DIRECTIONS FOR COMMUNITY COLLEGES, no. 74, Summer 1991 © Jossey-Bass Inc., Publishers

Tinto (1987) found that students' willingness to continue in college, when other things are equal, is related to their daily interactions with faculty outside of the classroom.

The story at Community College of Philadelphia (CCP) is one example of a college's efforts to approach the task of improving transfer opportunities through altering classroom practices, enriching the curriculum, and developing a supportive academic community. The college's approach also includes a strong faculty and student network between CCP and the major transfer institutions.

Building a Coherent Curriculum

The narration begins in 1983, when several deans of academic divisions and a small group of faculty attempted to address the seemingly incoherent course-taking behaviors of large numbers of students enrolled in the college's General Studies Program. This program developed in an atmosphere similar to many urban community colleges, where primary attention was given to access. Cohen and Brawer have described this preoccupation with access as resulting in students using the community college experience in ways that did not foster progression towards the baccalaureate.

Of equal concern to this group of professional staff at CCP was the intellectually limiting classroom practice of employing passive learning and requiring students merely to recall bits of information accumulated from classroom lectures and assigned readings. Understanding the problem as one that could not be resolved solely by redistribution of courses or by improved support services, this small group sought to use the power of curriculum as the centerpiece of any effort to improve transfer. Their effort resulted in the college's being one of six community colleges across the country to be awarded a Transfer Opportunity Grant from the Ford Foundation.

The Transfer Opportunities Program. A central element for the faculty of the Transfer Opportunities Program (TOP) is the common recognition that many students come from backgrounds that have not prepared them to appreciate or identify with academic life. They come with an understanding of education as simply a credentialing device earned by the accumulation of a defined number of credits. Their previous learning experiences leave them without adequate models of intellectual activity, and they often experience cultural conflicts when exposed to academic discussion requiring controversy and debate. Perhaps most importantly, many of the students come to the college lacking the community resources and educational prerequisites important to their chances for successful transfer.

The Transfer Opportunities Program offers students in General Studies an alternative to viewing college as "banking" a number of courses and credits and using whether or not they transfer to four-year colleges as the sole criterion. TOP sees the real educational task as preparing students to perform well at their transfer institution by replacing the independent, three-credit course with a twelve-credit unit of instruction staffed by a core group of faculty large enough to offer a vital intellectual community for students. The pedagogical approach mixes lectures with seminars, small-group discussion, "writing across the curriculum," and other activities that draw faculty and students into closer contact. Students can only take themselves seriously as learners if they enter into and experience the academic culture. Once they view themselves as members, they will be empowered to pursue academic goals beyond the community college.

Initially, TOP faculty engaged in three semesters of staff development activities. During the first semester, faculty teams met together to review texts and materials that were being proposed for use in the twelve-credit cluster. During the second semester the faculty team taught the cluster experimentally. The third semester was used as a reflection and refinement semester for evaluating the efforts of the second semester and for recommending changes.

Faculty teaching in TOP are required to renegotiate the norms of literacy by agreeing on the types of writing assignments, the uses to be made of primary texts, and the manner in which such texts are to be interpreted by students. As can be imagined, such agreements do not come easily and require weekly meetings to discuss student assignments and their relationship to learning objectives. They also require a special type of faculty member who is able to move beyond the confines of his or her individual classroom and consider teaching from the requirements of a broader curricular perspective.

During the first semester of study, full-time students are enrolled in a twelve-credit program, either *Introduction to the Social Sciences* or *Introduction to the Humanities*. During the social science semester students are scheduled as a group with four faculty members, three from the social sciences and one from English. In addition, student groups meet in counseling-mentoring seminars, team taught by a social science instructor and a counselor. During the humanities semester, four faculty work together with similar groups of students.

TOP is now ending its fifth year and has established itself as a small learning community within the broader General Studies Program. Since its inception in 1984, TOP has been serving between 70 and 160 students each semester with from three to five faculty teams. Preliminary study of the outcomes for minority students has been encouraging, but further, more in-depth analysis of both the quality of the educational experience and the longer-term outcomes is needed to help give future direction to the effort.

The TOP effort is only the beginning of the story of curriculum change at CCP. The most difficult challenge for any academic organization is moving forward from a small pilot effort at curricular reform to actually making significant changes for large numbers of students. The task is difficult enough when the focus is on the introduction of a new set of course requirements but becomes extremely complex when faculty are being asked to examine their classroom practices and agree to share a common pedagogical perspective. Add to this complexity the need to offer such a curricular experience for all learners—part-time and full-time, both on-campus and at community service sites—and the organization is faced with a monumental challenge.

From TOP Project to General Studies Curriculum Reform

In the summer of 1987, CCP began to mobilize its faculty with an intensive five-week planning seminar to design a coherent curricular structure for General Studies based partially on the experiences in the TOP and partially on those of other faculty engaged in the Humanities Enrichment Program funded by the National Endowment of the Humanities. The group agreed to the following basic principles of classroom practice that would be incorporated in any course developed or revised for the General Studies Program: use of original texts whenever possible, use of inquiry and interpretive skills, and requirement for critical writing and revision assignments.

At the urging of the college's president, the board of trustees agreed to provide institutional funding for staff and curriculum development over the five years of the project. Although the exact nature of the new curriculum is still being considered by the faculty at large, the General Studies Curriculum Committee is recommending the following elements as central to the curriculum:

Requirement to take a certain number of courses developed for General Studies and identified as critical thinking and writing courses

Core of courses required of all General Studies students to be selected from among various disciplines

Strong recommendation to take English composition and an entry-level math course upon entry into the college

Two semesters of the same science

Inclusion of national and international perspectives to help students broaden their vision to the global community

A coherent sophomore-level course of study to facilitate transfer

A summative seminar experience to foster the academic behaviors needed for successful transfer.

Building a Supportive Academic Environment

Equally as important as the development of a coherent curriculum to facilitate transfer is the involvement of students in a broader academic community. At CCP a supportive academic environment will start with the development of learning communities within the General Studies Curriculum. These communities will include students, counselors, faculty mentors, and learning-laboratory professionals all working together. Students attending full-time, for example, may be block-scheduled during the morning hours to accommodate their work schedules. They will be assigned classes with faculty in General Studies and will have access to other support professionals concerned about their learning. Students attending part-time in the evening at one of the regional centers will be encouraged to select General Studies courses over three or four semesters and will work with an identified group of faculty and students.

Building Curricular Bridges for Students. Encouraging students to enroll in four-year colleges and universities can be facilitated by providing a network between CCP and the transfer institutions. This network is being established by directly engaging CCP faculty and students with faculty from four-year institutions in several important ways.

Bucknell University and CCP have jointly undertaken a six-week summer program for predominantly minority at-risk CCP students. This program, modeled on the pioneering effort by LaGuardia Community College and Vassar College, brings twenty-five CCP students to the Bucknell campus. They take courses jointly developed and team-taught by faculties from both institutions. A similar program is operating between CCP and Beaver College. Again, this program serves predominantly minority students and is team-taught at the Beaver campus with faculty from the two colleges. CCP students attending either Bucknell University or Beaver College receive scholarships covering tuition, and room and board for the six-week programs of study. The goal of both these programs is to encourage minority-student transfer by providing a rich and rewarding summer experience.

A different approach to a summer-student experience is being carried out at Wilkes College in Wilkes-Barre, Pennsylvania. Four CCP minority students were recruited for a bridge program taking place over two summers on the Wilkes College campus. Students receive scholarships covering tuition, and room and board, and have opportunities for work-study jobs. The goal of this program is to recruit minority students from CCP for their junior year at Wilkes College by providing summer experiences to prepare them for transfer. Similar programs are being planned for CCP students with the state universities in Pennsylvania.

A grant from the Ford Foundation is enabling CCP to develop a series of seminars among two- and four-year college faculties to address introductory courses in the disciplines. These efforts have enabled CCP faculty to share their thinking with four-year faculty about courses being developed for the new General Studies curriculum core. The discussions have also opened the possibility for creative articulation agreements between CCP and the transfer institutions. Perhaps most critically, they have started cross-institution dialogues among two- and four-year faculty promising a new appreciation of the CCP student's academic and social needs and for the quality of the educational experience students are receiving at CCP.

The Central Role of Curriculum

The experiences of Community College of Philadelphia point to the central role of curriculum for improving transfer opportunities for students. Minority and other nontraditional students entering community colleges cannot be viewed simply as unadjusted or underprepared persons who need to be "improved" by support services so that they can enter the traditional classroom. The curriculum itself must be reformed to integrate the learning needs and cultural backgrounds of these students with professional notions of what constitutes an educated person. This reform can best be done when teachers, academic support staff, and students see themselves as part of the same community working towards shared understandings of learning goals. It calls for these same professionals to reconsider the nature of their work, and asks students to think differently about their involvement in and commitment to learning.

References

Cohen, A. M., and Brawer, F. B. *The Collegiate Function of Community Colleges: Fostering Higher Learning Through Curriculum and Student Transfer.* San Francisco: Jossey-Bass, 1987.

Rendón, L. I., and Nora, A. *Salvaging Minority Transfer Students: Towards New Policies That Facilitate Baccalaureate Attainment.* Cambridge: Massachusetts Institute of Technology, 1988. 39 pp. (ED 305 098)

Richardson, R. C., Jr., Fisk, E. C., and Okun, M. A. *Literacy in the Open-Access College.* San Francisco: Jossey-Bass, 1983.

Tinto, V. *Leaving College: Rethinking the Causes and Cures for Student Attrition.* Chicago: University of Chicago Press, 1987.

Aram L. Terzian is dean of the Division of Social and Behavioral Sciences and Human Service Careers, Community College of Philadelphia, Pennsylvania.

Progressive businesses have begun to take the diversification of their leadership seriously. Community colleges must follow suit.

Diversifying Leadership in Community Colleges

J. Richard Gilliland

Most countries of the world utilize only a small fraction of their human potential. Parts of Northern European countries, Canada, and the United States have begun to make use of the diverse leadership capabilities of women and persons of color and to recognize that they can and should play other than subordinate roles in responding to a planet consumed with the need for people who can create, organize, manage, and lead.

According to the report of the Commission on the Future of Community Colleges (Armes, 1988), new leaders for our institutions will require many of the skills previous leaders of community, technical, and junior colleges have had. In addition, they must be coalition builders, must be able to inspire others, and must have a well-developed and articulated sense of vision. Neither traditional leaders (older males in the United States and most of the rest of the world) nor any one subgroup of our diverse society possesses the full arsenal of leadership capabilities needed to face the challenges we now experience at the local, regional, national, and world levels.

This chapter covers five major areas:

1. Practical theory behind work force diversity
2. Ways that leadership diversity strengthens an organization
3. Progress currently being made with the diversification of leadership, both in higher education and in the private sector
4. Stages of the leadership-diversity cycle
5. Description of activities and progress toward accomplishing leadership diversity at Metropolitan Community College.

NEW DIRECTIONS FOR COMMUNITY COLLEGES, no. 74, Summer 1991 © Jossey-Bass Inc., Publishers

Practical Theory: Work Force and Leadership Diversity

First, within the more specific context of higher education, it is utterly senseless not to promote women and persons of color to roles of leadership at our institutions. The majority of community college students are women; should not women logically play a significant, even majority, leadership role in these institutions? Second, given the immense challenges our country faces, is it not good public policy to take advantage of as many diverse human resources as possible?

The inclusion of people with different gender and ethnic backgrounds in educational leadership and management roles provides added diversity to our institutions. In general systems theory, diversity is a natural property that allows for creativity and for the testing of new ideas. Pathways for program development and institutional innovation exist so that experiments can be evaluated against desired results, with the results being an even more diverse system.

More creativity and innovation result when the same logic is extended to include culturally varied people; people from a range of age groups, countries, and work experiences; people with differing sexual preferences and personality types. Most of us have not thought seriously about how our population differs or about what a wealth of backgrounds and experiences can offer to organizational leadership if unleashed. Such profound diversity is consistent with natural ecosystems (including human ones) that maximize what they do or create. The more points of view and the more references of experience there are, the more options that appear. Consequently, the more diverse the leadership team becomes.

The Value of Leadership Diversity to an Organization

Susan Wilke, the manager of internal affirmative action at Proctor and Gamble in Cincinnati, relates an example from the game Trivial Pursuit that describes in rather straightforward ways how valuable diversity can be to "winning" (personal interview, Oct. 1987). A demonstration she and others at Proctor and Gamble use to illustrate the power and potential of diversity involves playing Trivial Pursuit with two very different teams.

One team is selected with the criterion that its members be as homogeneous as possible. Team members are typically white, male, middle-aged, and similar in work and educational backgrounds. The competing team is as heterogeneous as possible—men and women, young and old, all possible racial and cultural backgrounds, wide differences in personality types, and greatly varied education and work experiences. The ensuing Trivial Pursuit game quickly shows that the diverse team brings much wider talents, experiences, and outlooks to the game. Collectively, the members know more and demonstrate a much stronger creative talent. They *destroy* the "sterile monocultural" team. Although this example perhaps oversimplifies the value of diversity, it provides a clear and concrete illustration of the importance of staff diversification to any organization.

Diversity produces stability, which is the ability of the system to withstand stress and to identify and respond to opportunities. In natural systems an example of stress might be an outbreak of corn-eating insects in a corn field. A corn field is a monoculture of plants, analogous to a white-male monoculture. The result for the corn field is near destruction of the entire ecosystem. An outbreak of an insect that eats one plant species in a rain forest will have very little effect on the entire ecosystem; a rain forest is the most diverse ecosystem known, analogous to a diverse social system. The rain forest is stable and dynamic; the corn field is not. Similarly, the diverse leadership team is both stable and dynamic; the monoculture is not. The diverse system has links to all parts of society, it has feelers out everywhere; it senses new needs, societal changes, problems, and opportunities.

Within community colleges, on the one hand, there are examples of institutions that have responded to the decline in numbers of recent high school graduates by diversifying their service spectrum. Community colleges that have widened their horizons and broadened their services to include customized training and programs and services for nontraditional populations have generally done well, as measured by enrollment stability and growth. On the other hand, community colleges that have not changed with the times, such as some private junior colleges, have watched with dismay as their student numbers and corresponding financial resources have dwindled.

A senior community college administrator, reflecting upon the continuing decline in student numbers at his institution, commented, "We have no new populations to pursue. The only new people here are from Indochina, and they don't speak English." Perhaps this administrator could have considered starting some English-as-a-Second-Language courses in order to begin the effective development of this new population that could benefit so much from a good community college.

For their part, public and private businesses and organizations have to a large extent committed themselves to affirmative action but have failed to understand the concept beyond affirmative action/equal employment opportunity programs (AA/EEO). As a result, qualified and capable persons of color and women may be hired but infrequently move up and too frequently leave, even after institutions have developed complex, expensive programs to recruit them in the first place.

In the office of Susan Wilke at Proctor and Gamble is a sign that states, "Convert Diversity from an Obligation to a Value." But as Roosevelt Thomas of the American Institute for Managing Diversity says, "It sure isn't easy" (personal communication, Sept. 1987). What is needed is an expanded vision of affirmative action that includes an appreciation of real cultural diversity as a strength and a richness characterizing the best leadership teams. This is easier said than done. Old ways of thinking have not considered the value of diversity. For example, Americans have grown up with a "melting pot" idea that implies a fusion of values, customs, languages, and cultures, rather than an appreciation for the qualities that make them different. The full potential of educational and business institutions will be realized more fully as they move beyond previous self-imposed limitations and benefit from real leadership diversity and richness.

Demographics may be a major factor in encouraging leadership diversity in the future, too. Nearly all the new work force in the next fifteen years in the United States will be women, people of color, and immigrants; at least 75 percent will come from these populations. An organization may not survive if it is still trying to force its employees into a narrow mold with traditional structures and rules; it may have to become multicultural.

Current Status of Leadership Diversity in Higher Education and the Private Sector

What kind of progress is being made on implementing leadership diversity? Most of the accomplishments are occurring in the private sector. Progressive companies are saying, "Diversifying leadership gives us a competitive edge. It's good business." However, this concept has not yet been recognized as a basic value in educational organizations.

The report of the Commission on the Future of Community Colleges calls for increased diversity of community college leadership. Although 35 percent of current administrators are women, only 10 percent of community college chief executive officers are women. According to the report, "Blacks and Hispanics are underrepresented among all administrative and faculty groups" (Armes, 1988, p. 42). Intensive recruitment of women and persons of color is called for, along with a long-term strategy of offering mentoring to new recruits.

Even businesses have a long way to go. In the private sector, Honeywell is considered highly progressive. Yet staff at the company's Minneapolis headquarters say that although Honeywell is addressing work force diversity, they believe much more needs to be done. Further, their perception is that no organization has met the mark. In many cases the organizations that have allowed the most change have done so only after what might be called "galvanizing" events. A class-action lawsuit or a takeover attempt is often the impetus for rapid cultural change. Using education, exposure, awareness, and behavior-modification techniques, Honeywell is hoping to alter employee attitudes (Copeland, 1988).

Companies and institutions attempting to diversify their work forces have at least two problems: (1) there are few experts to help because the field is new, and (2) there are few tools, except programs about topics such as Equal Employment Opportunity (EEO) laws and how to do an interview without violating EEO principles.

At Metropolitan Community College (Omaha, Nebraska), recognition of the importance of diversity evolved in a fairly logical way:

1. The leadership team worked hard at the basic AA/EEO activities and had some good initial successes.
2. Questions arose about how, with a student population consisting of 19 percent people of color and 58 percent women, MCC could effectively serve without similar demographics reflected in both faculty and staff.
3. The issue of fairness for women and persons of color was discussed.
4. These discussions led to more systematic thinking (inspired by the idea of diversity in natural ecosystems) and to corresponding applications to MCC's organizational systems and leadership directions.

Reviewing the literature and visiting companies that are diversifying their leadership have also helped develop our actions.

Before describing what Metropolitan Community College (MCC) has done, it is helpful to describe various steps that have been observed within other organizations attempting to create leadership diversity. Roosevelt Thomas of Morehouse College has studied organizational progress relating to this question; some of what follows is based on his observations.

Stages of the Cycle: Creating Leadership Diversity

Thomas (1986) describes some typical stages that have been observed in public and private institutions and organizations. First is the stage of problem recognition. Organizations find that a problem exists with their figures for either affirmative action or equal employment opportunity. The simple response they find is to increase the number of persons of color and women who are in the pipeline. Substantial outreach efforts are undertaken to find and hire women and ethnic minorities for available jobs, and increases do occur in employment of both populations in the entry-level manager positions. Significant evidence exists that these efforts will achieve the desired responses to the AA/EEO problem.

But then frustration begins. Company managers perceive that many of the new ethnic minorities and women employees do not seem to fit in well and are not becoming assimilated into the company or institutional culture. Apathy sets in. For the most part, women and persons of color simply accept the lack of professional movement; they sense that nothing can be gained by raising issues or concerns. Executives are quiet because they are baffled about the lack of organizational progress. In some cases crisis occurs. Governmental intervention and external special-interest-group pressure, combined with internal unrest on the part of women and persons of color, take place. Executives remain baffled. They feel that they have made a big effort and that all they have achieved is internal turmoil, the resignations of women and persons of color who were originally hired, and external pressures from regulatory agencies.

Thomas suggests new ways to break this cycle, a cycle that is observed too frequently. He encourages managers and executives to expand their focus and to begin the process of learning the values of employee diversity. He suggests clarification of the vision of where the organization needs to go. It is especially critical that the chief executive officer develop and expand his or her understanding to incorporate progressive thinking in regard to the diversification of leadership. This heightened sensitivity is extremely important to the success of organizations wishing to break the cycle of failure.

One area in the United States that has been seriously overlooked is that of developing acute intercultural listening skills. Thomlison (in press) describes tools and techniques that are quite useful to the practitioner who understands the need to work effectively with an expanding multicultural work force or student population. His ideas on multicultural listening skills are also of great value as we interact more and more with an increasingly sophisticated global economic and political environment.

Thomlison suggests that understanding some major components of culture can help improve intercultural listening, which includes such areas as values and beliefs, language, nonverbal codes, and cognitive processing. Although one's own cultural heritage cannot be set aside during cross-cultural encounters, communications and understanding can be greatly enhanced if there is awareness of some of the major dysfunctions and difficulties that may be present during intercultural communication. The ultimate goal of the cross-cultural communicator is to reduce uncertainties and misunderstandings whenever possible.

Changes in political, transportation, technology, and mass-communication systems bring people into more contact with those from other subcultures, cultures, and countries than at any other time in human history. The global community is shrinking, and intercultural contact is increasing in frequency as a result. Within the United States immigrants are arriving in greater numbers than ever before; two-thirds of the people in the world who are emigrating from one country to another are entering the United States.

Although it is not the purpose of this chapter to delve deeply into the subject of intercultural listening, the importance of developing this form of sensitivity to people different from ourselves should be emphasized. Kohls (1984) suggests starting with an understanding of the differences between typical values in the United States and those in other countries. Table 1 below provides some useful comparisons.

Table 1. Comparison of Values in the United States and Other Countries

Values in the United States	Values in Other Countries
Personal control over the environment	Fate
Change	Tradition
Time and its control	Human interaction
Equality/egalitarianism	Hierarchy/rank/status
Individualism/privacy	Group welfare
Self-help	Birthright inheritance
Competition	Cooperation
Future orientation	Past orientation
Action/work orientation	"Being" orientation
Informality	Formality
Directness/openness/honesty	Indirectness/ritual/"face"
Practicality/efficiency	Idealism/theory
Materialism/acquisitiveness	Spiritualism/detachment

Source: Kohls, 1984.

Related to the heightening of sensitivity and the development of intercultural listening skills is the process of creating an environment where no individual is either disadvantaged or advantaged because of race, gender, creed, sexual preference, or any other classification. The development of tolerance and openness are key characteristics to be sought in the creation of a progressive environment.

Current employees who may be predominantly middle-aged, white, and male must also be assisted to deal with the dynamics of pioneering. The development of an executive leadership and employee-diversity program involves the process of change. Such change will not occur overnight; thus, tenacity and planning are essential in order to achieve long-term positive results. Another important part of the process is the establishment of mentoring and nurturing processes for new employees. The problems experienced by organizations that approach leadership diversity in traditional ways—and thus limit the upward-mobility of their minority and women employees—result in part from the failure to create institutional programs and services, including ongoing staff development activities that help both new and long-term employees feel appreciated regardless of their cultural differences. To perpetuate an organization that does not value differences but encourages everyone to be alike is counterproductive. Such an approach dismisses the fact that different people bring a variety of values to an organization and are productive in different ways. Institutions must recognize that the greatest value individual employees can bring is their own special values, talents, and culture. Thus, the process of change should celebrate employee differences and find ways to capture and nurture these differences, to the benefit of both the organization and each individual.

Activities on Leadership Diversity

The following are programs or activities that were the initial building blocks of MCC's leadership diversity efforts. These approaches have been useful and effective at this institution, but each organization must develop its own programs to fit the specific needs and characteristics of its organizational climate:

1. *Formal Workshops.* There are a growing number of professional consultants who deal with issues of leadership and cultural diversity. Combined with talent within the institution or organization, such outside experts can be very important catalysts in bringing current issues to the attention of an organization's employees.

2. *Relevant Professional Meetings and Publications.* An increasing number of seminars and professional meetings are focusing on leadership and cultural diversity. The *Chronicle of Higher Education* is a good source of information, as are promotional mailings from meeting organizers.

3. *The Copeland-Griggs Videotapes.* This three-tape series, although designed for the private sector, is also quite appropriate for community colleges. Called *Valuing Diversity,* the series demonstrates many ideas that work. Four new tapes have been added recently (L. Griggs, personal interview, June 1989).

4. *Commitment by the Chief Executive Officer to the Values of Leadership Diversity.* Challenges to organizations, including community colleges, suggest a critical need for leaders who both understand and promote leadership diversity. A program to develop diversity will not get off the ground unless its values are espoused by the CEO and unless he or she perseveres in its acceptance and implementation. Both the requirement for new areas of competence in our leadership and the real impact of emerging demographics in the United States suggest strongly that community college leaders must embrace and value leadership diversity.

5. *Participation of Staff Members in Discussions Currently Under Way.* During the last two-year period, MCC staff have attended and/or participated in over twenty-five different programs targeting community college leadership and diversity. Important national and regional meetings are scheduled in the months ahead on this subject; these represent opportunities for leaders to learn more.

6. *Familiarity with Available Information.* Books, articles, speeches, and even surveys are now available on the subject of diversity. The serious community college leader must become familiar with this growing body of literature.

7. *Development and Promotion of Comprehensive Staff and Personnel Development Activities.* Most community colleges have formal staff development programs. Metropolitan Community College has used these planned periods for major activities on cultural and leadership diversity. Many sessions, both

small and large and using internal as well as outside resources, have helped to modify attitudes among most faculty and staff substantially.

The significant need for creative, new kinds of leadership strengths can be addressed by building a strong commitment to developing leadership diversity in organizations and institutions, including America's community colleges. Every available leadership resource must be utilized to assure the continued dynamism and relevance of America's community colleges. As we have already noted, the fact that at least three-fourths of the new work force will consist of women, persons of color, and immigrants suggests that demographic pressure will also compel diversification of leadership of our institutions.

In a recent issue of the *Daily Californian*, Brian Hill (1990, p. 3) wrote, "A tool box of only screwdrivers is not a good tool box no matter how excellent those screwdrivers may be." Community colleges face this challenge. Will they learn genuinely to value leadership diversity and implement processes and programs that will nurture a celebration of differences? It is clear that they must.

References

Armes, N. (ed.). *Building Communities: A Vision for a New Century*. Washington, D.C.: American Association of Community and Junior Colleges, 1988.

Copeland, L. "Valuing Diversity, Part I: Making the Most of Cultural Differences at the Workplace." *Personnel*, 1988, 65 (6), 22, 55–60.

Hill, B. "Marginal Utility." *Daily Californian*, Feb. 28, 1990, p. 3.

Kohls, L. R. "The Values Americans Live By." Unpublished paper, Meridian House International, 1984.

Thomas, R. *Managing Employee Diversity: Expanding the Scope of Equal Employment Opportunity/Affirmative Action*. Atlanta, Ga.: American Institute for Managing Diversity, Morehouse College, 1986.

Thomlison, T. D. "Intercultural Listening." In D. Borisoff and M. Purdy (eds.), *Listening in Everyday Life: A Personal and Professional Approach*. Lanham, Md.: University Press of America, in press.

Richard Gilliland is president of Metropolitan Community College in Omaha, Nebraska.

The college that does not make efforts in orientation and support will probably lose more minority faculty in the 1990s than it will gain.

Ten Steps to Successful Minority Hiring and Retention

Dale V. Gares, Exalton A. Delco, Jr.

It has been predicted that during the mid-1990s qualified faculty—and in particular, minority faculty—will not be available to fill teaching jobs at community colleges and universities. During this period, half the nation's professors will be approaching retirement, postsecondary enrollments will have increased, and minority students graduating at the master's and doctoral level will persist at the lower 10 percentile level (Mooney, 1990). The California community college system alone predicts it will need to hire eighteen thousand new faculty by 2005. Prospects for maintaining, not to mention increasing, minority faculty participation in the community colleges appear very bleak. Hiring minority faculty members in such areas as the physical sciences, engineering, and the life sciences will become even more difficult as a small percentage of the doctoral graduates in these fields are minorities (Carter and Wilson, 1989).

Over the past five years the Austin Community College (ACC) District in Austin, Texas, has executed a ten-step action plan aiming to hire minority faculty members in numbers proportionate to the central Texas ethnic populations. The program has been distinctly successful. Whereas the number of full-time minority faculty was 12 percent in 1985, by 1990 it had grown to 20 percent. These numbers are most impressive when we note that the number of minority faculty at ACC grew by 8 percent in five years while the national average for total full-time faculty at community colleges is 10 percent.

The district's success in minority recruitment, hiring, and retention is based on ten action steps.

Step 1. The first step has three parts. It starts with the *board of trustees.* The board must endorse the concept of affirmative action, pass a meaningful affirmative action policy, and then provide the necessary budgetary support to allow implementation. The second factor is administrative support, specifically, that of *the president*. Without the direct support of the president's office in monitoring the process, minority hiring practices are doomed. The president must be directly involved to see that the process works. Finally, support must come from the general *academic administration* of the college. These personnel must recognize the value of faculty, as well as student, ethnic diversity. The academic arm must be committed to the affirmative action policy as passed by the board and implemented by the president. This requires that the vice president of academic affairs, as well as the deans and the academic council, promote policies that will make it possible to recruit, hire, and train minority faculty and to conduct staff development for these faculty once they come on board.

Step 2. The second important step is the establishment of *a college plan*. The goals of this plan must be clearly stated, and they must be realistic. They must be objectives that most people can identify and recognize. The entire college personnel will know what the expectations are for affirmative action, will lend their support to those expectations, and will develop an atmosphere that is conducive to fulfilling the plan.

Once the plan is under way, a follow-up will be necessary. Follow-up should be on an ongoing basis designed to give timely feedback at regular intervals so that the college personnel on interview teams will not see large gaps between the time that a plan is implemented and goals are attained. Follow-up should be conducted at all stages of the hiring process, including orientation and staff development. College personnel should know what the hiring progress is, what the pitfalls are, and what has changed in the climate of the college or within the community or within the nation that would bring about a change.

It is important for administrative, as well as faculty, support groups to evaluate the progress of the college plan and ascertain the outcomes resulting from the affirmative action process. Just as important is the dissemination of those results so that the college personnel will know exactly how the plan is functioning, where it is both on and off track, and what their roles in the success have been.

Step 3. The third requirement is for *faculty support*. As long as the faculty are at odds with either the affirmative action plan or the college plan, neither will work. The affirmative action plan must be shared with faculty even before presentation to the board for approval; this participation will allow faculty to embrace the plan and attribute progress to their own efforts. They will be charged with the responsibility at the division or department level to see that their part of the plan is in accord with the college's commitment to minority faculty hiring. As part of the process, faculty will be responsible for formulating interview groups that will include minority faculty, a practice that will improve the hiring process.

Faculty will begin to see the payoff in higher minority-student retention and greater diversification, which is what the affirmative action plan should do for the college. The faculty will then support the plan even more than originally. The results, however, must be continually presented to the faculty. This feedback will permit faculty to recognize that there is progress and that there are advantages to having developed the plan.

Step 4. The fourth component is that of *recruiting*. Recruiting is now more important than ever because there are fewer qualified faculty, particularly minority faculty, for positions than there have been in the past. Increasingly, institutions are raiding each other's faculties for sought-after instructors, particularly minority members. For example, the California system has a minority hiring process funded by a state-created competition—both within and out of the state—for the same minority faculty. To deal with this situation, colleges must develop pipelines of direct access into college and university placement centers. Direct pipelines into graduate programs will allow administrators to talk individually with the instructors within those programs and with potential faculty members during their first year of graduate school. Administrators can begin to cultivate minority graduate students prior to their graduation by building a good relationship. This course of action depends on strong administrative support, a well-developed college plan, and faculty support for the affirmative action plan—all of which results in minority faculty being comfortable accepting positions at the college. The new minority faculty will inform other minority students (potential faculty) back at the colleges from which they were recruited. This approach continues to strengthen the pipeline.

A second element of recruiting is use of advertising, specifically, careful selection of those instruments that will provide coverage within the minority community, throughout the nation, and particularly within the college's region and state. To get the greatest advantage for the dollars spent, administrators must target specific publications. Advertising in one or two national publications such as the *Chronicle of Higher Education* is not sufficient. And administrators must be prepared to readvertise until the college obtains a representative pool containing minority applicants. A mistake often made is that of attempting to gain minority representation within the faculty with a nonrepresentative applicant pool. Of course, every pool does not have to be perfectly ethnically balanced, but consistent failure in this area will mean that the college will not meet its designed goals through the recruitment process.

A final consideration in recruitment is *personal communication*: direct contact with people who can put administrators in touch with qualified minority candidates. The value of this personal contact must not be underestimated. At Austin Community College the president, as well as the vice president of academic affairs and other top administrators, have traveled to many colleges, including historically black institutions and Hispanic colleges and universities. These trips were made to gain personal contact with prospective candidates and to encourage them to apply for faculty positions at the college. Local media resources are used to let individuals know of ACC's program, not only during the search process, but also on a continuous basis.

ACC uses the media to demonstrate gains and report its results. Public feedback can become an important recruiting tool later on to show that the community is supporting the college's effort. This helps to make applicants feel secure in joining the faculty ranks.

Step 5. The fifth step to hiring minorities is the *screening* of potential applicants. Many times minority individuals do not present themselves well on application forms. Committee members must carefully scrutinize specific qualifications for a job and not be misled by qualifications ancillary to the major thrust of the position being offered. The development of proper forms can keep the committee on track and individual members oriented to specific qualifications and guidelines to avoid screening people out on technicalities or inappropriate items. Committee members must be able to assess applicants based on relevant material and must seek those whose qualifications meet or most nearly approximate those needed for the faculty position. The committee should try to increase the minority participation within the pool of those to be interviewed, making it as heterogeneous a group as possible. Such a practice will enhance the chances of the college to reach its affirmative action goal.

Step 6. The sixth step is *the interview* itself. Requiring a teaching session during the interview has proven a sound strategy. First, it allows the committee to evaluate the person as a communicator, as a teacher, and as a knowledgeable individual. Second, it allows the individual to demonstrate skills in an area in which he or she is really prepared: that of being a teacher able to impart information to students. The committee can serve as students while the applicant presents a mini-teaching session.

Every question that is to be asked during the interview should be carefully reviewed by the entire committee. The questions should meet the criteria of the college's plan. The committee's consensus will ensure that interview questions assess more than one item of concern. Interview questions are often peripheral, trivial, and not clearly designed to analyze individual qualifications. The questions and the mini-lesson presentation allow an individual the freedom to demonstrate his or her ability in a nonthreatening environment.

During the interview process committee members must be aware of ethnic differences—those that surface as the applicant presents ideas or concepts. The committee must not judge an applicant inappropriately, based on its own expectations of appropriate Western cultural responses. The committee must make sure that it is not ruling applicants out because of perceptual differences. Finally, interviewers should seek to create an atmosphere that makes applicants feel welcome, at ease, and able to express who they are.

Step 7. The seventh step is *selection*. The selection process should not result in a rank ordering of the applicants. The selection committee should forward at least three names of qualified individuals that it feels would be assets to the teaching faculty at the college. The top-recommended applicants should then be reviewed by the academic deans and the vice president of academic affairs, who will then pass their names to the president with a recommendation for hiring. The president may or may not elect to interview the individuals but would have the ultimate authority to make the final decision. The process will have been fair, and the selection will have been representative of the applicant pool.

Reference checks should be carefully conducted. Bearing in mind the criteria used during the interview process, one then obtains a clear picture of the abilities, skills, and competence of an individual applicant.

The final stage of selection involves the president's decision. As a way of showing interest in the process, the president retains the final authority for selecting the person to be employed. This practice does not mean that the committee's recommendations do not count; the president simply keeps control so that he or she has the authority to indicate that the process did or did not meet the original goal. It may even be necessary to start over with a new search. In cases where the process must be repeated, those involved become aware that the president is truly committed to seeing that the college achieves its affirmative action goals and to using all reasonable means to increase the minority composition of the college's faculty.

Step 8. The eighth step is *orientation and support*. Immediately on arriving at the college, new faculty members should go through an orientation that exposes them to the college's culture, operations, and organization. New faculty should be assigned a seasoned faculty mentor who will help them through the first year. It is very important that the new faculty know the philosophy of the college, that they feel that it is a healthy atmosphere in which to work, and that they are comfortable within that environment.

Shortly after being assigned a mentor and undergoing orientation, all faculty members should be invited to a reception with the president and the academic officers of the college. The reception honors the new faculty and lets them know that they are important and welcome. New faculty members learn what their roles are and what expectations the academic community has. They learn subsequently of assignments to serve on committees that reflect their expertise or their disciplines. Quick assignment onto committees involves the new faculty immediately within the governance of the institution and facilitates their transition to the college. This orientation and support are a critical part of retaining faculty members. As hard as it is to recruit minority faculty members, retention can be an even greater problem. The college that does not make efforts in orientation and support will probably lose more minority faculty in the 1990s than it will gain.

Step 9. The ninth vital component is continued *staff development*. A staff development program based on faculty evaluations and addressing deficiencies, reinforcing strengths, and targeting special-interest seminars is essential. The college should also promote professional development for its faculty, particularly encouraging new faculty to attend conferences and workshops that build on their instructional strengths and upgrade and renew their skills.

Step 10. The final requirement for increasing minority representation within the faculty is *perseverance*. The institution must continually monitor its progress. A plan—no matter how noble—does not drive itself. The minute that anyone involved in implementing the plan lets up, the numbers will drop!

These ten steps to minority hiring and retention have been very successful for the Austin Community College District. If other colleges use them as we have, they will increase their minority participation and improve the quality of their instructional program.

References

Carter, D. J., and Wilson, R. *Eighth Annual Status Report on Minorities in Higher Education.* Washington, D.C.: American Council on Education, 1989.
Mooney, C. J. "Faculty Job Market Slowly Improving, Evidence Indicates." *Chronicle of Higher Education,* Apr. 18, 1990, pp. A1, 14–15.

Dale V. Gares is associate vice-president and Exalton A. Delco, Jr., is vice-president for academic affairs at Austin Community College, Austin, Texas.

What American higher education needs in the 1990s is to move the issue of rekindling minority participation to the top of our national, state, and institutional agendas.

Revitalization Efforts

Dan Angel, Adriana Barrera

In the late 1980s American higher education came to a disturbing realization: postsecondary institutions were simply not doing the job in terms of minority participation.

A 1986 report from the Education Commission of the States found that the "progress toward full participation of minorities in higher education has become distressingly stalled" (Mingle, 1987, p. 44). Wilson and Justiz noted in 1987 that the "once promising gains in minority recruitment at all levels of higher education had evaporated" (1987, p. 10). Robert H. Atwell, president of the American Council on Education, stated flatly that "we have hit the wall on minority participation. Since the early 80s we had seen a steady downturn in Black participation in education at every level after high school graduation and a snail paced growth in the abysmally low level of Hispanic participation" (American Council on Education, 1988a, p. 6). Finally, the Commission on Minority Participation in Education and American Life concluded that "the picture of stalled progress is dramatically clear. During the period when the pool of minority high school graduates was becoming bigger and better than ever, minority college attendance rates initially fell and have remained disproportionately low" (American Council on Education, 1988a, p. 11).

Leadership in isolating the issue of minority participation in higher education and focusing on ways to rekindle interest in it has largely come from three national higher educational associations: the American Council on Education (ACE), the Education Commission of the States (ECS), and the American Association of Community and Junior Colleges (AACJC).

NEW DIRECTIONS FOR COMMUNITY COLLEGES, no. 74, Summer 1991 © Jossey-Bass Inc., Publishers

American Council on Education

Although the ACE had established an office of minority concerns in 1981, it was not until February 1987 that the ACE's board of directors declared minority participation a priority issue and began a special minority initiative. Joining with the Education Commission of the States, the groups established the Commission on Minority Participation in Education and American Life. Gerald Ford and Jimmy Carter served as honorary co-chairs of the distinguished 37-member, blue-ribbon committee.

By May 1987 the committee released its report, *One-Third of a Nation*. This document did not equivocate: "America is moving backward, not forward, in its effort to achieve the full participation of minority citizens in the life and prosperity of the nation. . . . We deeply believe that now is the time for our nation to renew its commitment to minority achievement" (1988b, p. vii).

Also in 1988, the ACE Commission on National Challenges in Higher Education released its Memorandum to the 41st President of the United States (1988c). The document outlined critical decisions facing the incoming president of the United States. A key element of the report was the need for full minority participation.

In 1989 ACE published *Minorities on Campus: A Handbook for Enhancing for Diversity* (Green, 1989). The handbook was full of data sounding the alarm:

Between 1975 and 1985, black participation in higher education dropped from 48 percent to 44 percent
College attendance for Hispanics fell from 51 percent to 47 percent during that same decade
In 1985 only 16 percent of all college students were minority
Also in 1985, only 10 percent of the faculty and 12 percent of administrators were minority.

The handbook highlighted what ACE had learned about increasing minority participation in higher education over the previous two years as part of its minority initiative and provided practical suggestions and models of excellence for institutional use. Speaking of "lost momentum," the handbook urged colleges and universities to conduct an internal audit of their diversity climate. The handbook is a major breakthrough in its analysis of recruitment, retention, transfer, and related minority-participation issues.

Two other ACE publications in a series format have been instrumental in identifying, tracking, and urging action to revitalize minority participation. *Campus Trends, 1989* (El-Khawas) was the sixth in a series of higher education reports begun in 1984. Unlike prior reports it has a section entitled "Minority Initiatives" that lists some progress and some cause for alarm:

Four in five higher education institutions reported some level of activity to
   increase the enrollment and retention of minority students
Eight in ten administrators reported that activities were under way to
   improve the campus climate for minority students, but only half of the
   institutions regularly monitored attrition rates for minority students
Six in ten administrators rated their institutions as fair or poor in attracting black students
Seven in ten rated their institutions as poor in attracting Hispanic students.

   The best source for anyone interested in the plight and progress of
minority higher education is the annual series *Minorities in Higher Education*, prepared by the council since 1982. The eighth report (Carter and
Wilson, 1989, p. vi) noted, "Despite the efforts of some institutions and a
number of states to expand access to higher education for underrepresented racial and ethnic groups, we can only identify some pockets of
success."

Education Commission of the States

When the ECS joined with ACE in 1987 to create the Commission on
Minority Participation in Education and American Life, the organization
began a minority initiative of its own. ECS produced two major studies in
association with the State Higher Education Executive Officers: *Focus on
Minorities: Synopsis of State Higher Education Initiatives* (State Higher Education Executive Officers, 1987) and *Focus on Minorities: Trends in Higher
Education Participation and Success* (Mingle, 1987).
   The first report presents model initiatives in thirty-three states targeted
at minorities. The second report chronicles the progress toward full minority participation in higher education over a thirty-year period; it concludes
that "despite progress since the days of near exclusion, the full participation of minority students in our nation's colleges and universities remains
unrealized" (p. v). The second report also notes that college participation
immediately after high school fluctuates greatly among minority groups.
College attendance rates were 70 percent for Asian Americans, 51 percent
for whites, 46 percent for blacks, 38 percent for American Indians, and 37
percent for Hispanics (p. 9).
   In 1988 ECS released two more studies dealing with minority participation: *Serving More Diverse Students: A Contextual View* (Richardson, 1989a)
and *Institutional Climate and Minority Achievement* (Richardson, 1989b).
   The most significant ECS report from the community, vocational, and
technical-college point of view was released in June 1990: *Responding to
Student Diversity: A Community College Perspective* (Richardson, 1990). This
report reaches the both perplexing and challenging conclusion that "com-

munity colleges are part of the pipeline problem as well as the potential contributor to a solution" (p. 2).

In June 1989 the Education Commission of the States began an eighteen-month study of ways in which state governments could do a better job of recruiting and educating minority students. New Mexico's governor, Garey E. Carruthers, and Ohio's governor, Richard F. Celeste, co-chair the 24-member committee that will provide an action plan by 1991 (Cage, 1989).

American Association of Community and Junior Colleges

America's community, vocational, and technical college network has easily outdistanced the four-year universities in minority attendance. In 1988 44 percent of blacks and 54 percent of Hispanics began their higher education in a community college (American Council on Education, 1988d). Yet a comparison of fall 1976 and 1987 (see Table 1) enrollments indicates that the community college network has been more successful in gaining numbers than percentages (*Community College Times,* Jan. 31, 1989, p. 15).

Aware of the constancy of the percentages, the AACJC has been at work on the issue in a number of ways. In the summer of 1989, the fifty participants at the President's Academy in Vail, Colorado, listed the ten top challenges facing community, technical, and junior college leaders in the 1990s. The issue of minority concerns was second only to that of faculty development (Parnell, 1989). When the AACJC Board listed its six priorities for 1990, the need to launch a minority education initiative was at the top of the list (American Association of Community and Junior Colleges, 1989). Actually, the prominence of the minority issue was the result of several other efforts conducted by the organization. The AACJC's Minority Business

Table 1. Minority Enrollment in Community, Technical, and Junior Colleges, 1976 and 1987

Ethnic Groups	Fall 1976		Fall 1987	
	Number	Percentage of Total	Number	Percentage of Total
White	3,227,131	79	3,944,808	78
Black	449,348	11	505,745	10
Hispanic	285,948	7	354,021	7
Asian	81,699	2	202,298	4
American Indian	40,850	1	50,574	1
Total	4,084,976	100	5,057,446	100

Source: U.S. Dept. of Education and AACJC, 1987 ("AACJC Data File," 1989).

Enterprise Project, conducted in cooperation with the U.S. Department of Commerce, has granted more than $300,000 to campuses across the country. The AACJC also released an excellent report, *Minorities in Urban Community Colleges* (1988).

In 1990 the AACJC established a minority education initiative with an initial budget of $150,000 over a three-year period. Texas state representative Wilhelmina Delco chairs the thirteen-member commission. The commission met for the first time in May 1990 and decided to concentrate on a seven-point work plan: (1) Priority will be given to ethnic-minority students, faculty, and administrators. (2) Priority will also be given to college curriculum and staff development issues. (3) The December-January issue of AACJC's *Community, Technical, and Junior College Journal* will be devoted to ethnic minority concerns and will highlight exemplary practices at local colleges. (4) The commission will develop an action-oriented report. (5) The commission will conduct a hearing at the April 1991 AACJC Convention. (6) Coalitions will be developed with other organizations. (7) An awards program will be established to recognize selected individual colleges for exemplary minority programs (Commission on Improving Minority Education, 1990).

Councils and colleges affiliated with the AACJC are also involved in other efforts at securing more minority full-time faculty. In May 1989 the National Council of State Directors of Community and Junior Colleges published *The Dry Pipeline: Increasing the Flow of Minority Faculty* (Linthicum, 1989). According to this national study, only 10 percent of the faculty at two-year colleges in 1985 were minority: 4 percent black, 4 percent Asian, and 2 percent Hispanic, and Native American, respectively.

Another encouraging effort by the League for Innovation in the Community College and the Community College Leadership program at the University of Texas at Austin aims to develop ethnic-minority faculty members into mid-level college administrators. That multiyear effort is funded by a $926,000 grant from the W. K. Kellogg Foundation.

Quality Education for Minorities Project (QEM)

One other national study deserves mention among the leading efforts to revitalize minority participation in higher education: the QEM Project, initially based at the Massachusetts Institute of Technology. Under the chairship of former U.S. secretary of labor Ray Marshall, the project issued a 130-page report, *Education That Works: An Action Plan for the Education of Minorities* (Massachusetts Institute of Technology, 1990). Putting key emphasis on math, science, and engineering, the aim of the plan is to have minority students enroll in college in proportion to their share of the college-age population. That would mean at least one million more minority college entrants.

Encouraging Numbers

In the fall of 1988, total United States college enrollment topped 13 million for the first time in history. Minority enrollment hovered at 2.4 million (Evangelauf, 1990). Certainly these numbers are encouraging, but they cannot conceal the fact that the college attendance rate of black and Hispanic high school students has continued to trail that of whites.

The enrollment of various racial groups in two- and four-year institutions over the past decade is shown in Table 2 (Evangelauf, 1990, p. 1).

Demographics indicate that the number of minorities in the American population will increase dramatically in the future. One-third of the nation will be members of minorities by 2000; yet with all best efforts to date, only 18.4 percent of minority populations are enrolled in America's colleges.

As our research indicates, the history of the last decade is one of stalled progress and lost momentum. In the 1990s American higher education needs to move the issue of rekindling minority participation to the top of our national, state, and institutional agendas. With total rededication and a full commitment, we can go where we have been unable, unwilling, and undetermined to go before.

References

"AACJC Data File." *Community College Times,* Jan. 31, 1989, p. 15.

American Association of Community and Junior Colleges. *Minorities in Urban Community Colleges—Tomorrow's Students Today.* Washington, D.C.: American Association of Community and Junior Colleges, 1988. 34 pp. (ED 291 426)

American Association of Community and Junior Colleges. *AACJC Letter,* No. 333. Washington, D.C.: American Association of Community and Junior Colleges, 1989.

American Association of Community and Junior Colleges. Commission on Improving Minority Education, Minutes, May 7–8, 1990.

American Council on Education. *Annual Report 1988.* Washington, D.C.: American Council on Education, 1988a.

American Council on Education and Education Commission of the States. *One-Third of a Nation.* Washington, D.C.: American Council on Education, 1988b. 47 pp. (ED 297 057)

American Council on Education. *Memorandum to the 41st President of the United States.* Washington, D.C.: American Council on Education, 1988c.

American Council on Education. *The Minorities Initiative: A Special Update.* Washington, D.C.: American Council on Education, 1988d.

Cage, M. "Commission Begins Study of State Efforts to Educate Minorities." *Chronicle of Higher Education,* June 28, 1989, p. A16.

Carter, D. J., and Wilson, R. *Minorities in Higher Education: Eighth Annual Status Report.* Washington, D.C.: American Council on Education, 1989.

El-Khawas, E. *Campus Trends, 1989.* Washington, D.C.: American Council on Education, 1989. 84 pp. (ED 310 700)

Evangelauf, J. "1988 Enrollments of All Racial Groups Hit Record Levels." *Chronicle of Higher Education,* April 11, 1990, pp. A1, A36–A46.

Table 2. College Enrollment Trends by Race, 1978-1988

	1978	1980	1982	1984	1986	1988	10-year Change (in %)
American Indian:							
Four-year	35,000	37,000	39,000	38,000	40,000	42,000	+ 20
Two-year	43,000	47,000	49,000	46,000	51,000	50,000	+ 16
Asian:							
Four-year	138,000	162,000	193,000	223,000	262,000	297,000	+ 115
Two-year	97,000	124,000	158,000	167,000	186,000	199,000	+ 105
Hispanic:							
Four-year	190,000	217,000	229,000	246,000	278,000	296,000	+ 56
Two-year	227,000	255,000	291,000	289,000	340,000	384,000	+ 69
Black:							
Four-year	612,000	634,000	612,000	617,000	615,000	656,000	+ 7
Two-year	443,000	472,000	489,000	459,000	467,000	473,000	+ 7
White:							
Four-year	6,027,000	6,275,000	6,306,000	6,301,000	6,337,000	6,582,000	+ 9
Two-year	3,167,000	3,558,000	3,692,000	3,514,000	3,584,000	3,702,000	+17

Source: Evangelauf, 1990.

116   REKINDLING MINORITY ENROLLMENT

Green, M. F. (ed.). *Minorities on Campus: A Handbook for Enhancing Diversity.* Washington, D.C.: American Council on Education, 1989.

Linthicum, D. S. *The Dry Pipeline: Increasing the Flow of Minority Faculty.* Annapolis, Md.: National Council of State Directors of Community and Junior Colleges, 1989. 40 pp. (ED 307 912)

Massachusetts Institute of Technology. *Education That Works: An Action Plan for the Education of Minorities.* Boston: Massachusetts Institute of Technology, 1990. 139 pp. (ED 316 626)

Mingle, J. R. *Focus on Minorities: Trends in Higher Education Participation and Success.* Denver, Colo.: Education Commission of the States and the State Higher Education Executive Officers, 1987. 50 pp. (ED 287 404)

Parnell, D. "School Is In at President's Academy Workshop." *Community, Technical, and Junior College Times,* Aug. 1, 1989, p. 4.

Richardson, R. C., Jr. *Serving More Diverse Students: A Contextual View. Minority Achievement: Counting on You.* Denver, Colo.: Education Commission of the States, 1989a. 26 pp. (ED 318 365)

Richardson, R. C., Jr. *Institutional Climate and Minority Achievement.* Denver, Colo.: Education Commission of the States, 1989b.

Richardson, R. C., Jr. *Responding to Student Diversity: A Community College Perspective.* Denver, Colo.: Education Commission of the States, 1990.

State Higher Education Executive Officers and the Education Commission of the States. *Focus on Minorities: Synopsis of State Higher Education Initiatives.* Denver, Colo.: State Higher Education Executive Officers, 1987. 38 pp. (ED 287 403)

Wilson, R., and Justiz, M. "Minorities in Higher Education: Confronting a Time Bomb." *Educational Record,* 1987, *68* (4), 9–14.

Dan Angel is president of Austin Community College, Austin, Texas.

Adriana Barrera is assistant to the president at Austin Community College.

This chapter offers an annotated bibliography of ERIC documents and articles.

Sources and Information: Minority Participation in Community College Education

Grace Quimbita, Anita Y. Colby

Social trends, demographic changes, and labor-force development needs have revitalized efforts to increase minority participation and success in higher education. This chapter provides an annotated bibliography of the most recent ERIC literature dealing with minority recruitment and retention in American community colleges. Focusing on literature added to the ERIC database since spring 1989, the bibliography lists articles and documents concerned with minority access to education, student recruitment, programs and services designed to promote academic persistence, efforts to improve transfer rates and success, and state-level initiatives.

Access

Andrew, L. D., and Russo, R. "Who Gets What? Impact of Financial Aid Policies." Unpublished manuscript, 1989. 25 pp. (ED 309 717)

Focusing on changes in student financial aid, this article considers (1) the changes that have been made, (2) their effect on federal funding allocations and obligations, (3) ways these changes may have contributed to the growth of proprietary schools at the expense of community colleges, and (4) ways the changes may have resulted in the decline in Hispanic and African American participation in higher education.

Boyer, P. "The Tribal College: Teaching Self-Determination." *Community, Technical, and Junior College Journal*, 1989–90, *60* (3), 24–29. (EJ 404 259)

This article describes the growing number of community colleges chartered by American Indian tribes, located on reservations, and specifically designed to meet the educational and cultural needs of the American Indian community. The colleges' provision of culturally relevant curricula and training for cultural needs is highlighted, and the increasing need for state and federal support and for professional development is stressed.

California Community Colleges, Office of the Chancellor. *Annual Report on Extended Opportunity Programs and Services.* Sacramento: California Community Colleges, 1990. 15 pp. (ED 313 095)

This report to the state legislature by the Office of the Chancellor of the California Community Colleges evaluates the services provided by Extended Opportunity Programs and Services (EOPS). It also provides background on the twenty-year history of EOPS and identifies significant trends in EOPS enrollments, in student characteristics and goals, and in the utilization of program services.

DeLoughry, T. J. "For Junior College in Texas, U.S. 'Trio' Dollars Are Crucial. How the Billions of Dollars in the President's 1991 Budget Translate into Bread and Butter Issues at Six Colleges and Universities." *Chronicle of Higher Education,* February 7, 1990, pp. A25–26. (EJ 404 046)

This article recounts Southwest Texas Junior College's struggle to recruit and retain students from its impoverished service regions by stretching the federal dollars available through Upward Bound, Student Support Services, and other Education Department programs for disadvantaged students.

Kanter, M. L. "An Examination of Demographic, Institutional, and Assessment Factors Affecting Access to Higher Education for Underrepresented Students in the California Community Colleges." Paper presented at the annual meeting of the American Educational Research Association, Boston, Mass., Apr. 16–20, 1990. 48 pp. (ED 317 239)

This 1987 study investigates the extent to which demographic, institutional, and assessment factors affect the access of Hispanics, blacks, Native Americans, and students with disabilities to college-level courses. The study findings show that demographic and institutional characteristics related to race/ethnicity affected students' eligibility for transfer courses, associate-degree-applicable courses, or precollegiate basic-skills courses.

Rendón, L. I., and Taylor, M. T. "Hispanic Students: Action for Access." *Community, Technical, and Junior College Journal,* 1989–90, *60* (3), 18–23. (EJ 404 258)

This paper discusses the demographic and educational trends posing challenges at the nation's colleges and presents a ten-point plan to increase the participation, retention, and academic progress of Hispanic and other at-risk students.

Williams, C. "Broadening Access for Black Students." *Community, Technical, and Junior College Journal,* 1989–90, *60* (3), 14–17. (EJ 404 257)

This article focuses on the American Association of Community and Junior Colleges' Minority Education Initiative, which was based on an assessment of recent trends related to access, retention, and graduation rates of blacks in the educational pipeline. The article considers governmental issues, the teaching environment, the teaching and learning processes, and institutional effectiveness.

Recruitment

Anglin, L. W. "Preparing Minority Teachers for the 21st Century: A University-Community College Model." *Action in Teacher Education,* 1989, *11* (2), 47–50. (EJ 399 713)

This article describes a plan to recruit minority community college students into university-based teacher-preparation programs in order to address the nationwide shortage of minority teachers. The goal is to prepare thirty teachers per year to respond to local and national minority teacher shortages.

Arellano-Romero, O., and Eggler, J. *Recruitment, Retention, and Innovative Instructional Strategies for Culturally Diverse Minority College Students: A Review of the Literature.* Santa Barbara, Calif.: Office of Instruction, Santa Barbara City College, 1987. 77 pp. (ED 318 523)

This literature review focuses on the recruitment, retention, and teaching strategies for the culturally diverse student body at Santa Barbara City College in California. Chapters review the growing concern for the underrepresentation of Hispanics, blacks, and Native Americans in California's higher education systems; make recommendations concerning the recruitment and retention of minority students; feature innovative teaching strategies and curriculum case studies; and suggest areas for further research in learning assessment and audio-visual units.

Henninger, M. L. "Recruiting Minority Students: Issues and Options." *Journal of Teacher Education,* 1989, *40* (6), 35–39. (EJ 403 223)

This article examines selected basic assumptions that relate to minority-student recruitment into teacher education. Four categories of minority recruitment endeavors are discussed, and examples of each are provided.

Retention

Harris, Z. "Institutional Commitment to Cultural Diversity." *Community, Technical, and Junior College Journal,* 1989–90, *60* (3), 35–37. (EJ 404 261)

This article argues that the impact of growing cultural and ethnic diversity nationwide will have a pervasive impact on community colleges, and it emphasizes the importance of institutional reform and commitment to ethnic diversity. The characteristics shared by ten predominantly white colleges that have successfully retained and graduated large numbers of minority students are highlighted.

Miller, C. "Minority Student Achievement: A Comprehensive Perspective." *Journal of Developmental Education*, 1990, *13* (3), 6–8, 10–11. (EJ 405 825)
After reviewing statistics on current minority involvement in higher education, this article presents components of effective retention strategies. These include administrative commitment, financial resources, student services, curricula, personnel, and timeliness of intervention. A comprehensive approach to improve minority achievement and redefine matriculation expectations is suggested.

Riggs, R. O., Davis, T. M., and Wilson, O. H. "Impact of Tennessee's Remedial/Developmental Studies Program on the Academic Progress of Minority Students." *Community/Junior College Quarterly of Research and Practice,* 1990, *14* (1), 1–11. (EJ 405 829)
This article examines the impact of statewide mandatory testing and placement in Tennessee's community colleges on the retention and academic progress of minority students. It reports that attrition is higher for developmental students than for college-level students and higher for minority students than for white students. Few blacks enroll directly in college-level courses, and fewer still persist for three quarters.

Transfer

Ackermann, S. P. *An Analysis of Two UCLA Transfer and Retention Programs: The Transfer Alliance Program and the Supergraduate Program.* Los Angeles: Office of Academic Interinstitutional Research, University of California, Los Angeles, 1989. 38 pp. (ED 310 810)
A description is provided of the Transfer Alliance Program (TAP) and the Supergraduate Program, two transfer and retention efforts operating between the University of California at Los Angeles (UCLA) and local community colleges. TAP was created to promote the community college as a viable option for students seeking a baccalaureate degree and to encourage stronger academic preparation and curriculum planning in community colleges. The Supergraduate Program targets low-income and minority students in their junior year in high school and motivates and prepares them to pursue a college education.

California Postsecondary Education Commission. *Update of Community College Transfer Student Statistics, 1988–89: University of California, the California*

State University, and California's Independent Colleges and Universities. Commission Report 89-23. Sacramento: California Postsecondary Education Commission, 1989. 93 pp. (ED 313 073)

This report on the flow of transfer students from the California community colleges to the University of California and the California State University systems and to independent colleges and universities in the state focuses on transfer and articulation policy issues, trends in transfer among ethnic groups, and enrollment rates.

Farland, R., and Anderson, C. *The Transfer Center Project.* Sacramento: Office of the Chancellor, California Community Colleges, 1989. 42 pp. (ED 309 801)

This report describes California's Transfer Center Project, which was initiated to increase the number of community college students who transfer to four-year institutions, with particular emphasis on students from historically underrepresented groups. The report includes a description of the project, including information on transfer-center goals and operations, findings of an external evaluation, and a list of activities to be undertaken by the chancellor of the California Community Colleges to promote transfer.

Lieberman, J. (ed.). *The Pew Charitable Trusts: Center for At Risk Students.* Long Island City, N.Y.: LaGuardia Community College, 1989. 12 pp. (ED 315 107)

Three activities of LaGuardia Community College are described: the formation of the Center for At-Risk Students; the college's International High School, a collaborative program that serves high school students who are at high risk because of their limited English proficiency; and Exploring Transfer, a two-year/four-year college collaborative effort to increase the number of urban and minority transfer students.

Pincus, F. K., and DeCamp, S. "Minority College Students Who Transfer to Four-Year Colleges: A Study of a Matched Sample of B.A. Recipients and Non-Recipients." *Community/Junior College Quarterly of Research and Practice,* 1989, *13* (3–4), 191–219. (EJ 402 823)

This article describes factors promoting and inhibiting transfer and the attainment of bachelor's (BA) degrees. Findings are reported from interviews with forty-eight minority scholarship recipients who transferred from two-year to four-year colleges; BA recipients are compared with nonrecipients. Study findings are related to research on the importance of social integration into college life.

Watkins, B. T. "Community Colleges Urged to Bolster Liberal Arts to Help Students Transfer to Four-Year Institutions." *Chronicle of Higher Education,* November 1, 1989, pp. A35, 38. (EJ 399 257)

According to a report called *Bridges to Community* by the Academy for Educational Development and the College Board, between 15 percent and 25 percent of community college students transfer to four-year institutions. This article advocates that community colleges must make liberal arts programs their top priority if they are to help black and Hispanic students transfer.

Watkins, B. T. "Two-Year Institutions under Pressure to Ease Transfers." *Chronicle of Higher Education,* February 7, 1990, pp. A37–38. (EJ 404 042)

This article emphasizes that community colleges are being pressed to eliminate barriers that keep many students, especially minority students, from transferring to four-year institutions. The article mentions that over the last fifteen years community colleges have stressed occupational education and have not placed sufficient emphasis on academics.

Leadership

Academic Senate for California Community Colleges. *Contract Faculty Hiring Procedures: A Model Based on Assembly Bill 1725.* Sacramento: Academic Senate for California Community Colleges, 1989. 9 pp. (ED 315 140)

This policy statement on contract-faculty employment includes sections on hiring philosophy, affirmative action, position identification, search procedures, selection-committee procedures, and statement review and revision. The report lists qualifications desired in applicants, including sensitivity to and understanding of the diverse academic, socioeconomic, cultural, and ethnic backgrounds of community college students.

Sheehan, M. C. *Faculty and Staff Diversity Update: A Report.* Sacramento: Office of the Chancellor, California Community Colleges, 1990. 32 pp. (ED 313 093)

This quarterly report by the Faculty and Staff Diversity Unit of the chancellor's office of the California Community Colleges presents the 1988–89 objectives of the unit and the actions taken to meet them. The progress report provides information on expenditures, increases in underrepresented group applicants and hires, colleges targeted for recruitment efforts, districts' self-evaluations of outcomes, ongoing funding requirements, and specific activities that did and did not have expected results.

Vaughan, G. B. "Black Community College Presidents." *Community College Review,* 1989, *17* (3), 18–27. (EJ 407 346)

This article discusses survey responses from seventeen of forty-eight black community college presidents who were polled regarding their paths to the presidency, their job interviews, the assets and liabilities associated with being a black candidate for the presidency, affirmative action, mentors and role models, negative role models, and racial aspects of the presidency.

Vaughan, G. B. *Leadership in Transition: The Community College Presidency.* Riverside, N.J.: American Council on Education/Macmillan Publishing Company, 1989. 146 pp. (ED 311 960)

This book examines issues currently facing community college presidents and argues for a change in leadership to meet the needs of a new era in higher education. Two chapters draw from survey data to consider the special problems and advantages of women, black, and Hispanic presidents.

Vaughan, G. B. *Pathway to the Presidency: Community College Deans of Instruction.* Washington, D.C.: American Association of Community and Junior Colleges, 1990. 228 pp. (ED 318 526)

Written to enhance the understanding of administrators, faculty members, and board members regarding the position of dean of instruction at community colleges, this book reports and analyzes study findings on the background, preparation, and roles of people in this position. Included is a separate survey of female, black, and Hispanic deans.

Revitalization

American Association of Community and Junior Colleges. "1990 AACJC Public Policy Agenda." *Community, Technical, and Junior College Journal,* 1990, *60* (4), 45–47. (EJ 407 338)

This article presents the six goals adopted by the American Association of Community and Junior Colleges as priorities for 1990: minority education initiative, leadership development, institutional effectiveness, human resource development, international/intercultural education, and federal relations.

Connecticut State Board of Higher Education. *Recruitment and Retention of Minorities in Connecticut Higher Education: A Status Report.* Hartford: Connecticut State Board of Higher Education, 1989. 22 pp. (ED 311 759)

Connecticut's Strategic Plan for Racial and Ethnic Diversity was created in 1985 to increase minority participation in the state's higher education system through recruitment and retention. This report presents a model for examining the progress in the implementation of the plan. It also includes data on specific minority-group enrollments and percentages of minorities at the undergraduate, graduate, and professional levels. Degree awards to minorities are tracked. The report concludes that the state is exhibiting progress in minority recruitment and that the improvement of retention should be further emphasized.

"Eight States Develop 'Bold' Programs to Increase Minority Graduation Rates." *Black Issues in Higher Education,* 1989, *5* (23), 1, 10. (EJ 399 903)

A national competition for the design of model programs to help more minorities graduate from four-year colleges and universities has resulted in grants to Arizona, Colorado, Illinois, Massachusetts, Montana, Ohio, New York, and Tennessee. This article outlines state plans to develop articulation agreements, transfer, computerized tracking, cooperatives, and financial incentives.

New Mexico Commission on Higher Education. *Planning for the Class of 2005: A Vision for the Future. The Strategic Plan for Higher Education in New Mexico.* N.p.: New Mexico Commission on Higher Education, 1988. 61 pp. (ED 313 072)

This long-range plan for higher education in New Mexico is a guide for decision making rather than a plan for individual colleges. Introductory sections explain the development of the plan; planning principles and assumptions; conclusions about economic development, demography, and education in New Mexico; and goals, priorities, and the future. Among the plan's thirty-two policy statements are directives for the improvement of minority participation in higher education, including statements on financial incentives for improved participation; on professional shortages; on costs, tuition, and financial aid; and on developmental education, diversification of the delivery of education, and statewide course articulation.

Wittstruck, J. R., Hess, R. J., and Stein, R. *Challenges and Opportunities: Minorities in Missouri Higher Education.* Jefferson City: Missouri Coordinating Board for Higher Education, 1988. 57 pp. (ED 310 821)

An overview is provided of the issues related to the participation and retention of minorities in higher education in Missouri and across the nation. The appended paper, "Trends and Issues of Minority Participation in American Higher Education," examines high school graduation and college participation rates, the transition from high school to college, minority enrollment in undergraduate and postgraduate education, community college transfers, recruitment and retention in four-year institutions, minority-faculty role models, campus climate, institutional support services, and faculty recruitment and retention trends.

Grace Quimbita is a staff writer for the ERIC Clearinghouse for Junior Colleges.

Anita Colby is associate director of the Clearinghouse.

INDEX

Academic practice, 82–85
Academy for Educational Development, 121–122
Access, 8, 117–119; barriers to, 19, 31–38; educational quality issues and, 25–28, 28, 32, 88; institutional level challenges to, 16–18; legal basis for, 23–24; socioeconomic changes and, 24–25, 39; trends and issues in, 23–25, 28
Accreditation agencies, 73, 82
ACE. See American Council on Education (ACE)
Achieving a College Education (ACE), 20
Ackermann, S. P., 120
Adams v. Richardson, 69
Adelman, C., 79–80, 85
Adjustment to higher education, student, 21
Administration. See Personnel, community college
Advertising, 41–42, 105
Affirmative action/equal opportunity (AA/EEO), 94–97, 103–108
American Association of Community and Junior Colleges (AACJC), 3, 81, 109; Minority Education Initiative, 113, 119; public policy agenda, 48, 54, 72, 112–113, 123
American Council on Education (ACE), 72, 83, 109; Minorities in Higher Education annual reports, 1–2, 111, 114; One-Third of a Nation, 13, 110, 114
American Indian students: programs for, 49–54, 117–118; statistics on, 48–49, 111, 115
American values, 99
Ames, N., 96, 101
Anderson, C., 121
Andrew, L. D., 117
Anglin, L. W., 119
Archer, E., 79, 80, 86
Arellano-Romero, O., 119
Articulation agreements: with four-year postsecondary institutions, 11, 19, 26–27, 34, 53–54, 74, 81, 91; with secondary school systems, 11, 43–44,

49. See also Connections, institutional; Transfer
Articulation factors, 17, 70–71, 121, 124
Asian Americans, 1, 95, 111, 115
Assessment: of the campus environment, 35–36; of faculty applicants, 106–107, 122–123; of minority programs, 60–61; of students, 17, 50–51
Associate degrees, 2, 74
Associations (higher educational), roles of, 109–114. See also Names of organizations
Astin, A. W., 24, 25, 29
Atwell, R. H., 4, 109
Austin Community College (ACC) District, 103–104

Bakke case, 24
Barriers: to access, 31–38, 71–72; educational environment, 71–72; institutional, 16–18, 35; language, 32, 43, 48, 51, 95; overcoming, 33–35; public policy, 18–19; racism and prejudice, 32, 36, 73–74; to recruitment, 33–35; to transfer, 17–18, 73, 82, 122
Beaver College, 91
Bender, L. W., 53, 54, 55, 72, 73, 75, 81–82
Birnbaum, R., 23, 25, 28, 29
Black college presidents, 122, 123
Black Student Opportunity Program (Florida), 26–27
Black Student Retention Program (Maryland), 58–60
Black students: access by, 29, 119; statistics on, 2, 40, 57, 110, 111, 115
Board of Trustees for Connecticut Community-Technical Colleges, 41, 46
Boyer, P., 117–118
Brawer, F. B., 84–85, 87, 88, 92
Bridges between schools. See Connections, institutional
Bridges to Community, 121–122
Brint, S., 79, 80, 85–86
Bucknell University, 91
Bureau of Indian Affairs, 48
Business education, 52

125

ORDERING INFORMATION

NEW DIRECTIONS FOR COMMUNITY COLLEGES is a series of paperback books that provides expert assistance to help community colleges meet the challenges of their distinctive and expanding educational mission. Books in the series are published quarterly in Fall, Winter, Spring, and Summer and are available for purchase by subscription as well as by single copy.

SUBSCRIPTIONS for 1991 cost $48.00 for individuals (a savings of 20 percent over single-copy prices) and $70.00 for institutions, agencies, and libraries. Please do not send institutional checks for personal subscriptions. Standing orders are accepted.

SINGLE COPIES cost $15.95 when payment accompanies order. (California, New Jersey, New York, and Washington, D.C., residents please include appropriate sales tax.) Billed orders will be charged postage and handling.

DISCOUNTS FOR QUANTITY ORDERS are available. Please write to the address below for information.

ALL ORDERS must include either the name of an individual or an official purchase order number. Please submit your order as follows:
    Subscriptions: specify series and year subscription is to begin
    Single copies: include individual title code (such as CC1)

MAIL ALL ORDERS TO:
    Jossey-Bass Inc., Publishers
    350 Sansome Street
    San Francisco, California 94104

FOR SALES OUTSIDE OF THE UNITED STATES CONTACT:
    Maxwell Macmillan International Publishing Group
    866 Third Avenue
    New York, New York 10022

Other Titles Available in the
New Directions for Community Colleges Series
Arthur M. Cohen, Editor-in-Chief
Florence B. Brawer, Associate Editor